D0731652

CELTIC
NAMES

CELTIC NAMES

THEIR MEANING, HISTORY AND MYTHOLOGY

SEAN MCLAUGHLIN

ARCTURUS

ARCTURUS

This edition published in 2011 by Arcturus Publishing Limited
26/27 Bickels Yard, 151–153 Bermondsey Street,
London SE1 3HA

Copyright © 2011 Arcturus Publishing Limited

All rights reserved. No part of this publication may be reproduced,
stored in a retrieval system, or transmitted, in any form or by any means,
electronic, mechanical, photocopying, recording or otherwise, without
prior written permission in accordance with the provisions of the
Copyright Act 1956 (as amended). Any person or persons who do any
unauthorised act in relation to this publication may be liable to criminal
prosecution and civil claims for damages.

ISBN: 978-1-84858-045-9
AD001911EN

Printed in Singapore

CONTENTS

INTRODUCTION

IN COMPILING this collection of Celtic names, it has become clear to me that any such glossary would lack relevance without at least a basic understanding of the history of the people from whom the names originate. When you read through the origins and explanations of the names contained within, you will come across frequent references to spear carriers, charioteers, cattle, beauty, saints etc. What is the significance of these references? In order to appreciate the meaning behind so many Celtic names, it is necessary to know a bit about the Celts themselves.

Of all the great peoples of whom history gives account, few can match the charisma of the Celts. Today the popular view of them is of a fair-skinned, fair-haired race that blended a passion for warfare with a love of art; a romantic, hot-blooded, dexterous, creative, mystical people, who were ultimately driven to the farthest corners of north-western Europe, where they have preserved their culture to this day in the face of repeated oppression.

While some aspects of this modern view of the Celts are accurate, the whole story is far more complicated. For a start, the Celts cannot be described as a race; rather, they appear to have formed a collection of autonomous tribes, whose customs and appearance varied, but whose common link was a language, albeit one of differing forms. What's more, it was a language used for speech rather than writing; while the Celts left a rich legacy of jewellery, metalwork, stone carving and other crafts, they left nothing in the way of written accounts to tell us exactly who they were, where they came from and how they lived their lives.

The importance of names

What we do know of the Celts has come to us from three sources: the descriptions by Greek and Roman writers, themselves only observers at best, and prone to put their own interpretation on what they saw as the Celtic way of life; archaeological finds, which have told us a great deal and continue to reveal more; and names. Celtic names found on coins and appearing amongst the Latin inscriptions on stone and metalwork, as well as existing Celtic place names, have provided a link between the surviving Celtic languages – Irish, Scots Gaelic, Manx, Welsh, Cornish and Breton – and the ancient language that gave the Celts their original identity.

That the true identity of the Celts remains something of a mystery, though, only adds to their charisma. And as archaeologists and linguists continue to piece together the evidence that is gradually bringing the picture into focus, a fascination and proud preservation of Celtic culture continues to be observed, not only in the British Isles – the last bastion of Celtic culture in Europe – but also in places across the globe, such as America and Australia, where descendants of the Celtic hordes that once migrated to Britain, themselves migrated in the last 300 years.

So what do we know about the Celts? The first strong traces of a Celtic culture date back to the 5th century BC. As the Bronze Age gave way to the Iron Age, the Celts had become masters of working iron and other metals, such as gold, into weapons, jewellery and ornaments. Artefacts from this period show the Celts to have occupied an area of Europe to the north of the Alps, between Burgundy and Bohemia, which rapidly spread to what is now northern Spain and Portugal, up through France to Britain, and west as far as Turkey.

As well as being highly accomplished craftsmen, these people were farmers, raising crops and livestock, with cattle being a symbol of wealth. They formed tribes ruled by kings, their royal lines running from king to grandchild. Hence, in Ireland for example, we find the naming reference O', meaning descendant of. In Old Irish this was written 'Uí', as in Uí Brien (grandson of Brian). It was this powerful and wealthy ruling class that gave the Celts their stereotypical image of massively built, fair-haired warriors with wild facial hair. This is how they are depicted in the accounts of the Greeks and Romans, who would have seen them on the battlefield, often naked, their bodies painted blue and their hair plastered back with lime wash, which accentuated their fair appearance, especially by contrast to the soldiers from the Mediterranean countries.

Much of the Celtic way of life would have been peaceful, raising their farms, making their artefacts and trading, but it is their exploits on the battlefield that attracted most attention. And when it came to battle, they were a fearsome foe. Warlords were carried around on chariots and their charioteers assumed exalted status. They were highly skilled drivers, careering across the battlefield in all directions, instilling fear in the enemy, before pulling up behind their own lines so that the warrior lord could lead his men into battle on foot.

In the 4th century BC their warlike nature spilled out across Europe, culminating in the brutal sacking of Rome. The Romans knew them as 'Galli' (from which we get Gauls), the Greeks as 'Keltoi'. They were without doubt the predominant force in Europe at that time.

Driven out of Europe

But it didn't last. Having withdrawn from Rome in exchange for ransom, they opened the door to their own downfall. By the 2nd century BC, the Celts were being squeezed in mainland Europe by the forces of Rome on the one hand and of Germania on the other. Their strength was concentrated in Gaul, and, when Julius Caesar completed his conquest in 52 BC, the last flames of Celtic culture in mainland Europe were effectively snuffed out.

In the British Isles, however, the Celts continued to thrive. Though the Romans eventually overpowered the resistance put up by the British Celtic tribes under the leadership of first Caratacus and then Boudicca, their presence in Britain over the next 500 years had little effect on the Celtic social structure or the Celtic language. Instead, it was a period of relatively peaceful co-existence, with the Romans forming pacts with one Celtic tribe in order to gain protection against another.

Such political manoeuvring is typical of the Celtic era and shows that this was not one race, as such, nor a single empire, but a conglomeration of groups of varying sizes, some gaining dominion over others, with territories expanding and contracting and allegiances shifting.

Two languages

The movement of the Celts in the British Isles is also interesting. Looking at the geography of surviving Celtic culture today – Ireland, Wales, the Scottish Highlands, Cornwall and Brittany – it is easy to assume that the Celts were driven back as one by the Roman advance, until they occupied nothing more than the western fringes of the British Isles. But this is not the case. For a start, the Irish Celts were of a different origin to those in mainland Britain, with a different version of the language: Goidelic as opposed to Brithonic. Of the Celtic languages still in use today, Irish, Scots Gaelic and Manx are derived from Goidelic, Welsh, Cornish and Breton from Brithonic.

The term 'Goidelic' comes from 'Goídel', itself a form of the Welsh name for the Irish, Gwyddel. In the 3rd and 4th centuries AD, Irish Celts invaded parts of Wales, north-western England and Scotland. Later, when Welsh missionaries made the journey the other way, they took the name Gwyddel to Ireland, where it became Goídel and Goidelic, hence Gaelic. This is just one example of the complex etymology of Celtic words and names, and gives an idea why many names have more than one possible origin.

Another group of Irish Celts who settled in parts of western Britain were those known as the *Scotti* – not a tribal name but a nickname, meaning raiders or plunderers. The *Scotti* settled in Scotland, but their name was not applied to that country until seven centuries later. In fact, the Latin name *Scotia* was originally applied to Ireland. It was the *Scotti* who brought the Gaelic tongue to Scotland and established Gaelic culture in the Highlands, which would later become the Kingdom of the Scots.

Meanwhile, the Irish invaders in Wales had been counteracted by the Romans implanting settlers from the Celtic Votadini tribe, moving them from the north-east of England to north Wales, where they became the ruling power in Wales, united the people of that country under the name Cymru (countrymen), and established the Welsh royal dynasty.

But it wasn't until the arrival of the Anglo-Saxons in Britain in the 5th century AD that the name Wales was used. For Wales and Welsh are derived from the Saxon word 'wealisc', meaning strangers, which they applied to anyone living beyond the scope of their conquest, including Devon and Cornwall. Thus personal names derived from Welsh, such as Walsh, are really Anglo-Saxon in origin, even though the people who first bore them were usually Celts.

Just as the Celtic settlements in the British Isles were the result of much toing and froing, rather than a linear withdrawal, the Celtic element in Brittany, in north-western France, is not the last vestige of the Gauls, who dominated France in the last three centuries BC. Instead, the Breton Celts came across the English Channel from south-western Britain, from Devon, Cornwall and Wales, over a period of two centuries following the Saxon invasion of England. Initially they would have been fleeing the Saxon onslaught, but later there would have been an exchange of trade and Christian missionaries maintaining links between the Celts of Brittany, Cornwall and Wales.

The Christian era

The spread of Christianity sparked an era in which Celtic culture flourished in its remaining homelands. Christian missionaries like St Patrick brought writing, and so began a process of putting the story of the Celts down in ink on paper. Up until then, with the exception of the Greek and Roman observations, Celtic law and folklore had been passed down by word of mouth. This was the work of the druids, a combination of scholars and mystics, who carried the real power among the Celts.

While the missionaries spread Christianity throughout Ireland, and into the furthest corners of Celtic Britain and Brittany, it became a major influence on Celtic culture. But while the Celts abandoned paganism and adopted 'Christian' names, they also applied their own art to the spread of Christianity. Ireland was now the hotbed of Celtic culture. Untouched by Roman and Saxon invaders, embraced by Christian evangelists, the distinctive Celtic style, which had arrived more than a thousand years earlier, flourished and spread, to the point where it became once more an influence in mainland Europe.

Even the Viking invaders in the 8th century had little impact on Celtic culture, but as the Celtic lands gradually became absorbed into Britain in the late Middle Ages and beyond, their language and customs began to disappear. Economic disasters, such as the Irish potato famine of 1840, saw large numbers of Irish and Scots migrating across the Atlantic to America, and further to find new homes in Australia and New Zealand.

Thus the Celtic story spread all around the globe, and with the threat of extinction of Celtic culture came a renewed determination to keep the old customs and language alive. Thus the language lives on, most vigorously in Wales and Ireland, as well as parts of Scotland and Brittany. Meanwhile, the Celts continue to spread, just as they always did, in diffuse pockets, united by a common, indefinable sense of historic identity.

Celtic mythology

The Celts were a religious people whose gods were fearsome characters. In order to stay on the right side of them, the Celts held feasts and ceremonies designed to appease the gods, offering sacrifices of animals and sometimes humans.

Many Celtic names are derived from the myths that grew around these deities, passed down from generation to generation, in songs and poems by the druids or bards. With the coming of Christianity, these myths and legends started to be written down, but the earliest surviving manuscripts date from around the 11th century AD. Thanks to these medieval writers, the Celtic legends live on today, romanticized somewhat perhaps, but no doubt founded in the very stories that were recited amongst the ancient Celts.

The Irish cycles

Throughout this book you will find references to Cu Chulainn, Fionn Mac Cool, Queen Medb, Conchobar Mac Nessa, Brian Boru and other legendary Irish figures. These are all characters that appear in the four cycles of Irish folklore: the Mythological Cycle, the Ulster Cycle, the Fenian Cycle and the Historical Cycle.

The first is the Mythological Cycle, which comprises stories of the Celtic gods and the origin of the people of Ireland. It tells of the goddess Danu and her people, the Tuatha Dé Danann, who held dominion over Ireland before the arrival of the Celts. When the Gaels settled in Ireland, the Tuatha Dé Danann became fairy people, occupying the Celtic underworld, and the tales depict them as a mixture of deity and royalty.

In this cycle we encounter characters such as the Mórrigán and the Dagda, two of the Celts' most powerful gods, along with Lugh, Brigid and Boann, the goddess of the River Boyne.

The Ulster Cycle is based in a later age and tells of the triumphs and tragedies of the Ulaid warrior people of Ulster and their rivals from Connacht. There are duels, battles and numerous feats of cattle rustling, interlaced with magic and mystery. The most famous character is Cu Chulainn (or Cúchulainn), son of Lugh, who is a warrior of superhuman strength with a tendency to fly into a terrifying and uncontrollable rage in battle.

The climax of the Ulster Cycle is the Cattle Raid of Cooley, in which Cu Chulainn goes into battle against the entire army of Connacht to prevent their Queen Medb from stealing a sacred bull, in order to win a bet with her husband Ailill.

Other legendary characters from the Ulster Cycle include Cu Roi, a king of Munster, and Deirdre of the Sorrows.

While the Ulster Cycle centres on Ulster and Connacht, the Fenian Cycle turns the focus of Irish mythology on to Leinster and Munster, and the exploits of Fionn Mac Cool (or Fionn Mac Cumhail). We meet Bradan Feasa, the Salmon of Knowledge, who lives in the Well of Wisdom, and who, by accident, passes on all the knowledge in the world to Fionn Mac Cool.

Fionn Mac Cool leads an army, the Fianna, against his enemy Goll Mac Morna, in a heroic cycle of fighting, hunting and venturing into the world of the spirits. The Ulster Cycle features two of Ireland's most well-known legends, Oisin in Tir na nOg and The Pursuit of Diarmuid and Grainne, the latter thought to be the origin of the tale of Tristan and Iseult.

Finally comes the Historical Cycle, in which myth makes way for fact. This is a collection of tales contrived by court poets to entertain their kings with tales of their own dynastic past. Here we find the great king Brian Boru, scourge of the Dublin Vikings and founder of the O'Brien clan.

In all these tales we find a characteristic that is evident throughout Celtic history: the mixture of savagery and martial heroism with artistry and romance. These contrasting passions are also to be found in the Welsh myths.

The Welsh Mabinogion

That the most comprehensive collection of Welsh myths and legends was given its name by a lady of the English aristocracy may seem incongruous, but Lady Charlotte Guest, daughter of the 9th Earl of Lindsey, was a leading 19th-century authority on Welsh literary history and her translation of medieval Welsh manuscripts, the Mabinogion, remains the leading source of Welsh mythology today.

The name comes from the four main stories in the text, known as the Four Branches of the Mabinogi, each of which ends with the words, 'thus ends this branch of the Mabinogi.' Lady Charlotte believed the name meant something along the lines of 'stories for children'.

The Four Branches of the Mabinogi are tales of magic, love, cunning and vengeance, recounting the exploits of a group of inter-related heroes and heroines. They begin with Pwyll, Prince of Dyfed, in which we meet Arawn, ruler of the Annwn, the Otherworld (or Heaven), Pwyll's wife Rhiannon and their son Pryderi.

Pryderi then figures in the other three branches: Branwen, Daughter of Llyr; Manawydan, Son of Llyr; and Math, Son of Mathonwy.

The original sources for the Mabinogion were two manuscripts dating from the 14th century, the *Red Book of Hergest* and the *White Book of Rhydderch*. These books in turn drew from songs and poems recounted in the Dark Ages, when Saxon supremacy in Britain would have suppressed much of the Welsh literary culture. This makes it hard to say when these legends actually originated, but there are other stories in the Mabinogion that offer a suggestion that much of it is based on historical fact.

In addition to the Four Branches, the Mabinogion consists of five traditional Welsh stories and three romances. Amongst these tales are references to the legend of King Arthur, a figure who has assumed mythical status over the centuries, but who was, it seems, a very real figure.

The Arthurian legend

Of all the Celtic tales to have survived to modern times, the one that outshines them all is the legend of King Arthur. This Celtic king of the Britons has fired the imagination of numerous prominent writers, each of whom has embellished the tale with his own imaginative twists, to the point where Arthur is portrayed as a magical character, chivalrous and romantic, a far cry from the original warrior king who led the people of Romano-Britain into bloody battle with the Saxons.

But the early accounts of Arthur tell it like it is. From the Welsh poets Taliesin and Aneirin, who lived in the 6th and 7th centuries AD, we get a picture of the true brutality that characterized the Saxon invasion, and the ferocity of the British warlords who fought to repel it. And they tell us that chief among those lords was Arthur.

Over the years, tales of Arthur's prowess in battle gather momentum, so that by the 9th century, the Welsh monk Nennius writes that Arthur killed 960 of the enemy single-handed at the battle of Badon Hill, the last of his victories and the battle that was said to have halted the Saxon advance.

But the Arthurian legend really took wing in the 12th century, thanks to two writers who breathed new life into the story. The first was the Welsh cleric Geoffrey of Monmouth, who chronicled the lives of past kings of Britain in his *Historia Regum Britanniae* (History of the Kings of Britain). One of his subjects in the *Historia* was Arthur, and Monmouth's account gives us a first contact with a number of the characters and plots that have become central to the Arthurian legend today. Merlin, Uther Pendragon, Guinevere, Excalibur, Tintagel, Avalon; none of these details are found in any account of Arthur before *Historia Regum Britanniae*, but that is not to say that Geoffrey of Monmouth made them up.

A few years after Monmouth wrote his account, a French court poet named Chrétien de Troyes added more flourishes to the legend of King Arthur, most importantly the Knights of the Round Table and the quest for the Holy Grail. De Troyes introduced us to Lancelot and Perceval, adding Gallic flair to Monmouth's account, turning the names from Welsh to French, and sending the story galloping forward with a liberal sprinkling of chivalry, magic and heroic adventure.

By the time Thomas Mallory published *Le Morte d'Arthur* (the Death of Arthur) in English in 1485, with the help of William Caxton and his printing press, the legend had become a work of popular fiction. The fabulous story of the illegitimate son of King Uther Pendragon, who proved his nobility by pulling a sword out of a stone, became king, with Merlin his court magician, married the beautiful Guinevere and fought against his nephew Mordred and the treacherous sorcery of his sister Morgan Le Fey; the formation of the Knights of the Round Table, their quests for the Holy Grail, Guinevere's adultery with Lancelot, the death of Arthur and the returning of his magical sword Excalibur to the Lady of the Lake – all this had become a medieval fairy tale.

But at its foundation lay a fantastic reality – the true story of the people known as the Celts.

GIRLS' NAMES A–Z

An alphabetical list of all the Celtic girls' names listed in this book and the chapter in which they can be found.

Aamor	*Personality traits*	Airic	*Personality traits*
Aednat	*Personality traits*	Aislin	*Physical features*
Aela	*Personality traits*	Aislinn	*Physical features*
Aelwen	*Physical features*	Aithne	*Personality traits*
Affraic	*Personality traits*	Alana	*Personality traits*
Afric	*Personality traits*	Alane	*Personality traits*
Africa	*Personality traits*	Alanna	*Personality traits*
Aibhilin	*Roles*	Alannah	*Personality traits*
Aibhlinn	*Roles*	Alastrina	*Roles*
Aibrean	*Events*	Alastrine	*Roles*
Aibreann	*Events*	Alastriona	*Roles*
Aideen	*Personality traits*	Aleen	*Physical features*
Aigneis	*Personality traits*	Aleena	*Physical features*
Ailbe	*Personality traits*	Aleine	*Personality traits*
Ailbhe	*Physical features*	Alena	*Physical features*
Aileen	*Personality traits*	Alice	*Personality traits*
Ailene	*Personality traits*	Alina	*Physical features*
Ailidh	*Personality traits*	Aline	*Physical features*
Ailis	*Personality traits*	Allena	*Physical features*
Ailish	*Personality traits*	Allene	*Physical features*
Ailsa	*Physical features*	Alma	*Personality traits*
Aina	*Personality traits*	Almeda	*Physical features*
Aine	*Personality traits*	Almha	*Personality traits*
Aineislis	*Personality traits*	Alys	*Personality traits*
Aingeal	*Personality traits*	Amena	*Personality traits*

Anabla	*Physical features*	Argante	*Personality traits*
Anchoret	*Personality traits*	Argantlon	*Physical features*
Andraste	*Personality traits*	Argantlowen	*Physical features*
Andreva	*Roles*	Ariana	*Physical features*
Aneira	*Personality traits*	Arianrhod	*Physical features*
Angharad	*Personality traits*	Arienh	*Personality traits*
Annaic	*Personality traits*	Arlana	*Personality traits*
Annaig	*Personality traits*	Arleen	*Personality traits*
Annick	*Personality traits*	Arlene	*Personality traits*
Annowre	*Personality traits*	Arleta	*Personality traits*
Anwen	*Physical features*	Arlette	*Personality traits*
Aobh	*Physical features*	Arlina	*Personality traits*
Aobhinn	*Physical features*	Arline	*Personality traits*
Aoibheann	*Physical features*	Armelle	*Personality traits*
Aoibhell	*Physical features*	Arzhela	*Physical features*
Aoife	*Physical features*	Ashling	*Physical features*
Aouregan	*Physical features*	Athract	*Events*
Aouregwenn	*Physical features*	Avenie	*Places*
Aphria	*Personality traits*	Awena	*Roles*
Ardanata	*Personality traits*	Azenor	*Personality traits*
Arden	*Personality traits*	Aziliz	*Physical features*
Ardena	*Personality traits*	Baibin	*Roles*
Ardene	*Personality traits*	Beatha	*Personality traits*
Ardra	*Personality traits*	Becuma	*Personality traits*
Arela	*Roles*	Bedelia	*Physical features*

Beibhinn .... *Physical features*	Branna .... *Physical features*
Benalban .... *Roles*	Brannagh .... *Physical features*
Berched .... *Personality traits*	Branwen .... *Physical features*
Berit .... *Physical features*	Breage .... *Physical features*
Berneen .... *Physical features*	Breched .... *Personality traits*
Berta .... *Physical features*	Breed .... *Personality traits*
Betha .... *Personality traits*	Breeda .... *Personality traits*
Bethan .... *Personality traits*	Brenda .... *Physical features*
Betrys .... *Roles*	Brendana .... *Roles*
Bevin .... *Physical features*	Brenna .... *Physical features*
Birgit .... *Physical features*	Bret .... *Places*
Birkita .... *Physical features*	Bretta .... *Places*
Birte .... *Physical features*	Briaca .... *Personality traits*
Blaine .... *Physical features*	Briallen .... *Physical features*
Blair .... *Places*	Briana .... *Personality traits*
Blaithin .... *Physical features*	Briann .... *Personality traits*
Blanaid .... *Physical features*	Brianna .... *Personality traits*
Blathnaid .... *Physical features*	Briannah .... *Personality traits*
Bleuzenn .... *Physical features*	Brianne .... *Personality traits*
Blodeuwedd ...... *Physical features*	Briannon .... *Personality traits*
Blodwen .... *Physical features*	Brid .... *Personality traits*
Boadicea .... *Roles*	Bride .... *Personality traits*
Boann .... *Physical features*	Bridget .... *Personality traits*
Boudicca .... *Roles*	Bridie .... *Personality traits*
Brangaine .... *Physical features*	Brienna .... *Personality traits*

Brienne ....*Personality traits*

Brietta ....*Personality traits*

Brighid..............*Personality traits*

Brigid ....*Personality traits*

Brigitta ....*Personality traits*

Brigitte ....*Personality traits*

Brina ....*Roles*

Brisen...............................*Roles*

Brit .... *Places*

Brita .... *Places*

Brite ....*Personality traits*

Brites ....*Personality traits*

Britta ....*Personality traits*

Brittany .... *Places*

Brona ....*Personality traits*

Bronagh............*Personality traits*

Bronte ....*Personality traits*

Bryana ....*Personality traits*

Bryann ....*Personality traits*

Bryanna ....*Personality traits*

Bryanne ....*Personality traits*

Brygid ....*Personality traits*

Brynna .... *Places*

Caera................................*Roles*

Caireann ....*Roles*

Cairistiona ....*Roles*

Caitlin ....*Personality traits*

Caitriona...........*Personality traits*

Camryn .... *Physical features*

Caoilainn .... *Physical features*

Caoilfhinn......... *Physical features*

Caoimhe .... *Physical features*

Cara...................................*Roles*

Caragh ....*Roles*

Carey................*Personality traits*

Caronwyn..........*Personality traits*

Cary ....*Personality traits*

Cassidy .... *Physical features*

Cathbodua........................*Roles*

Catriona............*Personality traits*

Ceasg................*Personality traits*

Ceinlys..............*Personality traits*

Ceri ....*Personality traits*

Ceridwen ....*Roles*

Cessair..............*Personality traits*

Ciara................. *Physical features*

Cigfa................. *Physical features*

Cinnia .... *Physical features*

Cinnie .... *Physical features*

Claire .... *Physical features*

Clarisant	*Physical features*	Dana	*Places*
Cliodhna	*Physical features*	Dara	*Physical features*
Cliona	*Physical features*	Darcy	*Physical features*
Clodagh	*Places*	Darfhinn	*Physical features*
Cobhlaith	*Personality traits*	Dearbhail	*Roles*
Coinchend	*Events*	Dearbhorgaill	*Roles*
Coleen	*Roles*	Dechtire	*Roles*
Colleen	*Roles*	Dee	*Personality traits*
Cora	*Roles*	Deheune	*Personality traits*
Cordelia	*Personality traits*	Deirdre	*Roles*
Coventina	*Roles*	Delbchaem	*Roles*
Creiddylad	*Personality traits*	Delia	*Physical features*
Creidne	*Personality traits*	Demelza	*Places*
Creirwy	*Personality traits*	Deniela	*Personality traits*
Crisiant	*Personality traits*	Deoch	*Roles*
Cruatha	*Personality traits*	Derryth	*Personality traits*
Crystal	*Personality traits*	Deva	*Personality traits*
Crystyn	*Roles*	Devona	*Personality traits*
Cyhyreath	*Personality traits*	Dilic	*Personality traits*
Dacie	*Personality traits*	Dilys	*Personality traits*
Dailigh	*Places*	Dindrane	*Personality traits*
Daimhin	*Personality traits*	Diorbhail	*Personality traits*
Daire	*Physical features*	Diva	*Personality traits*
Daireann	*Physical features*	Divone	*Personality traits*
Damhnait	*Roles*	Dogmaela	*Personality traits*

Doireann...........*Personality traits*

Domhnacha......................*Roles*

Donalda ....*Roles*

Donella ....*Roles*

Donia .... *Physical features*

Doreen ....*Personality traits*

Doreena ....*Personality traits*

Drusilla ....*Personality traits*

Duana .... *Physical features*

Dubh Lacha...... *Physical features*

Duibheasa......... *Physical features*

Duibhghiolla .... *Physical features*

Dwyn ....*Personality traits*

Dwynen ....*Personality traits*

Dymphna ....*Personality traits*

Eabha ....*Personality traits*

Eachna ....*Personality traits*

Eadain ....*Personality traits*

Eadaoin.............*Personality traits*

Ealasaid.............*Personality traits*

Ealga ....*Personality traits*

Edana ....*Personality traits*

Edna ....*Personality traits*

Eibhleann .... *Physical features*

Eibhlin .... *Physical features*

Eileen .... *Physical features*

Eilis....................*Personality traits*

Eilwen .... *Physical features*

Eimear .... *Physical features*

Eimhear ....*Personality traits*

Einin .... *Physical features*

Eirwen.............. *Physical features*

Eithne ....*Personality traits*

Eitna.................*Personality traits*

Elaine ....*Personality traits*

Elara .... *Places*

Elen ....*Roles*

Elsha ....*Personality traits*

Eluned .... *Physical features*

Emer .... *Physical features*

Ena .... *Physical features*

Enat...................*Personality traits*

Enda..................*Personality traits*

Engl ....*Personality traits*

Enid...................*Personality traits*

Enora ....*Personality traits*

Enya ....*Personality traits*

Epona...............................*Roles*

Erea .... *Places*

Erena................*Personality traits*

Erie	*Places*	Finnguala	*Physical features*
Erin	*Places*	Finola	*Physical features*
Erina	*Places*	Fiona	*Physical features*
Ertha	*Personality traits*	Fionnuala	*Physical features*
Erwana	*Roles*	Fionnula	*Physical features*
Esyllt	*Physical features*	Firinne	*Personality traits*
Etain	*Personality traits*	Flaitheas	*Personality traits*
Ethne	*Physical features*	Flanna	*Physical features*
Eubha	*Personality traits*	Fódhla	*Places*
Eurielle	*Personality traits*	Frann	*Personality traits*
Eurwen	*Physical features*	Franseza	*Places*
Evelina	*Personality traits*	Gael	*Places*
Eveline	*Personality traits*	Ganieda	*Personality traits*
Evelyn	*Physical features*	Gaynor	*Physical features*
Fanch	*Places*	Gearoidin	*Personality traits*
Fainche	*Personality traits*	Genevieve	*Physical features*
Fedelma	*Personality traits*	Germaine	*Physical features*
Feenat	*Personality traits*	Gethan	*Physical features*
Fenella	*Physical features*	Gilda	*Personality traits*
Ffion	*Physical features*	Gildas	*Personality traits*
Fflur	*Physical features*	Ginebra	*Physical features*
Fianna	*Roles*	Ginerva	*Physical features*
Fidelma	*Personality traits*	Ginessa	*Physical features*
Findabair	*Physical features*	Giorsal	*Physical features*
Fingula	*Roles*	Gitta	*Physical features*

Gladez .... *Places*

Glenda .... *Personality traits*

Glenys .... *Places*

Gobhnet............ *Physical features*

Gormflaith .... *Roles*

Gormla............................... *Roles*

Gormlaith .... *Roles*

Gormley .... *Roles*

Grainne .... *Personality traits*

Grania .... *Personality traits*

Granuaile .... *Roles*

Guenevere .... *Physical features*

Guennola .... *Physical features*

Guinevere .... *Physical features*

Gunoda .... *Personality traits*

Gwen .... *Physical features*

Gwencalon .... *Physical features*

Gwendolen ...... *Physical features*

Gwendolyn .... *Physical features*

Gwendydd......... *Personality traits*

Gweneira........... *Physical features*

Gwener.............. *Personality traits*

Gweneth .... *Physical features*

Gwenith .... *Physical features*

Gwenllian.......... *Physical features*

Gwenneth .... *Physical features*

Gwenonwyn ...... *Physical features*

Gwenyver .... *Physical features*

Gwyndolin .... *Physical features*

Gwyneth............ *Personality traits*

Gwynith .... *Personality traits*

Gwynne .... *Physical features*

Hafwen.............. *Physical features*

Haude .... *Personality traits*

Hayley .... *Events*

Heilyn .... *Roles*

Helori .... *Personality traits*

Heodez .... *Personality traits*

Heulwen .... *Personality traits*

Hieretha........... *Personality traits*

Ia .... *Physical features*

Idelisa .... *Personality traits*

Idelle .... *Personality traits*

Igerna................ *Physical features*

Imogen .... *Roles*

Ineda................. *Physical features*

Inira .... *Personality traits*

Iona................................. *Places*

Ione .... *Physical features*

Irnan .... *Roles*

Iseabal .... *Personality traits*	Kendra .... *Personality traits*
Iseult .... *Physical features*	Kennocha .... *Physical features*
Isolde .... *Physical features*	Kerenza .... *Personality traits*
Isolt .... *Physical features*	Keri .... *Physical features*
Ivori .... *Physical features*	Kerry .... *Physical features*
Janet .... *Personality traits*	Kew .... *Personality traits*
Jannet .... *Personality traits*	Keyne .... *Physical features*
Jennifer .... *Personality traits*	Kiera .... *Physical features*
Jenny .... *Physical features*	Kira .... *Physical features*
Jennyfer .... *Physical features*	Kirstie .... *Personality traits*
Jennyver .... *Physical features*	Klervi .... *Personality traits*
Jocelyn .... *Roles*	Koulm .... *Personality traits*
Joyce .... *Roles*	Koulmia .... *Personality traits*
Judwara .... *Roles*	Kristen .... *Personality traits*
Kacee .... *Personality traits*	Kyla .... *Physical features*
Kady .... *Roles*	Kyna .... *Personality traits*
Kaitlin .... *Personality traits*	Kyra .... *Physical features*
Kanna .... *Personality traits*	Laban .... *Physical features*
Katell .... *Personality traits*	Lachtna .... *Physical features*
Keela .... *Physical features*	Lana .... *Physical features*
Keelia .... *Physical features*	Laorans .... *Places*
Keelin .... *Physical features*	Lara .... *Personality traits*
Keely .... *Physical features*	Lasair .... *Physical features*
Keera .... *Physical features*	Lavena .... *Personality traits*
Keira .... *Physical features*	Lena .... *Personality traits*

Lesley	*Places*	Maire	*Personality traits*
Leslie	*Places*	Mairead	*Physical features*
Levenez	*Personality traits*	Mairi	*Personality traits*
Lileas	*Personality traits*	Maiwen	*Physical features*
Linette	*Personality traits*	Malvina	*Physical features*
Linnet	*Personality traits*	Maolisa	*Personality traits*
Linnette	*Personality traits*	Marc'harit	*Physical features*
Liobhan	*Physical features*	Marella	*Places*
Llian	*Physical features*	Marilla	*Places*
Loeiza	*Roles*	Marsali	*Physical features*
Luighseach	*Physical features*	Marvina	*Personality traits*
Luiseach	*Physical features*	Maureen	*Physical features*
Lynet	*Personality traits*	Mavelle	*Personality traits*
Lynette	*Personality traits*	Mavie	*Personality traits*
Lyonesse	*Personality traits*	Mavis	*Personality traits*
Mab	*Personality traits*	Mavourna	*Personality traits*
Maban	*Personality traits*	Meadghbh	*Physical features*
Mabina	*Physical features*	Meadhbh	*Personality traits*
Macha	*Roles*	Meara	*Personality traits*
Madailein	*Personality traits*	Medb	*Personality traits*
Madenn	*Personality traits*	Melle	*Personality traits*
Madrun	*Personality traits*	Melva	*Physical features*
Maebh	*Personality traits*	Melvina	*Physical features*
Maeve	*Personality traits*	Meredith	*Roles*
Maeveen	*Physical features*	Merewin	*Personality traits*

Meriel .... *Places*

Merna .... *Personality traits*

Meryl .... *Places*

Mikaela .... *Personality traits*

Miniver.............. *Physical features*

Mirna .... *Personality traits*

Moina .... *Personality traits*

Moira .... *Personality traits*

Mona................. *Personality traits*

Monca.............................. *Roles*

Mór .... *Personality traits*

Moreen .... *Personality traits*

Morgan .... *Places*

Morgana .... *Places*

Morgance .... *Places*

Morgane .... *Places*

Morna .... *Personality traits*

Morrigan ....*Roles*

Morvana .... *Physical features*

Morwenna.......................*Roles*

Moya................. *Personality traits*

Moyna .... *Personality traits*

Muireann........................ *Places*

Muirenn.......................... *Places*

Muirgheal .... *Places*

Muirne .... *Personality traits*

Muriel .... *Places*

Mwynen............. *Personality traits*

Myfanwy .... *Personality traits*

Myrna .... *Personality traits*

Naible............... *Personality traits*

Nanna .... *Personality traits*

Nara .... *Personality traits*

Nareen .... *Personality traits*

Nareena .... *Personality traits*

Nareene .... *Personality traits*

Navlin............... *Personality traits*

Neala ....*Roles*

Nealie ....*Roles*

Neasa................ *Personality traits*

Nemetona......... *Personality traits*

Nerys ....*Roles*

Nessa .... *Personality traits*

Nesta .... *Personality traits*

Nevena............. *Personality traits*

Nevidd............................. *Places*

Nevina.............. *Personality traits*

Nevitt.............................. *Places*

Niamh .... *Physical features*

Nodhlaig..........................*Events*

Noirin .... *Personality traits*

Nola................... *Physical features*

Nollaig .... *Events*

Nolwenn .... *Personality traits*

Non .... *Personality traits*

Noni .... *Roles*

Nora .... *Personality traits*

Norah............... *Personality traits*

Noreen.............. *Personality traits*

Nuala................. *Physical features*

Nuline .... *Personality traits*

Oanez................ *Personality traits*

Oifa .... *Personality traits*

Oighrig .... *Physical features*

Olwen............... *Physical features*

Olwyn .... *Physical features*

Oona .... *Personality traits*

Oonagh............. *Personality traits*

Orchil................ *Physical features*

Oriana .... *Physical features*

Orla.................. *Physical features*

Orlagh............... *Physical features*

Orlaith .... *Physical features*

Ornait .... *Physical features*

Ove .... *Personality traits*

Padraigin .... *Personality traits*

Padriga .... *Personality traits*

Paola .... *Personality traits*

Penarddun .... *Physical features*

Piala .... *Personality traits*

Radha............... *Physical features*

Raghnailt .... *Personality traits*

Regan .... *Personality traits*

Reghan.............. *Personality traits*

Rhedyn.............. *Personality traits*

Rhegan.............. *Personality traits*

Rhian .... *Roles*

Rhiannon........................... *Roles*

Rhianwen.......... *Physical features*

Rhonwen........... *Physical features*

Riona................. *Personality traits*

Rionach............. *Personality traits*

Rivanon .... *Roles*

Riwanon .... *Roles*

Roisin .... *Physical features*

Ronana .... *Personality traits*

Ronat .... *Personality traits*

Rosaleen .... *Physical features*

Rosmerta............................ *Roles*

Rowen .... *Physical features*

Rowena .... *Physical features*	Shibley .... *Personality traits*
Rozenn.............. *Physical features*	Shona .... *Personality traits*
Ruari .... *Physical features*	Sian .... *Personality traits*
Ryanne .... *Roles*	Sibeal .... *Roles*
Sadh .... *Personality traits*	Sile .... *Physical features*
Sadhbh.............. *Personality traits*	Sine .... *Personality traits*
Saoirse............... *Personality traits*	Sinead .... *Personality traits*
Saraid .... *Personality traits*	Siobhan............. *Personality traits*
Scathach .... *Physical features*	Siomha.............. *Personality traits*
Seasaidh .... *Personality traits*	Sorcha .... *Personality traits*
Seirial .... *Physical features*	Steren................ *Physical features*
Seirian............... *Personality traits*	Sterenn .... *Physical features*
Selma .... *Personality traits*	Sulgwenn .... *Personality traits*
Senga .... *Physical features*	Taillte .... *Personality traits*
Seonag .... *Personality traits*	Tamsin .... *Roles*
Seonaid .... *Personality traits*	Tangwystl .... *Personality traits*
Sererena............ *Personality traits*	Tara .... *Places*
Seva .... *Roles*	Teagan .... *Physical features*
Seve .... *Roles*	Teagin .... *Physical features*
Shanley .... *Roles*	Teamhair......................... *Places*
Shauna .... *Personality traits*	Tegan .... *Physical features*
Sheelagh .... *Roles*	Tegwen.............. *Physical features*
Sheena .... *Personality traits*	Tierney.............. *Personality traits*
Sheenagh .... *Personality traits*	Trifin .... *Personality traits*
Sheila .... *Physical features*	Trifine .... *Personality traits*

BOYS' NAMES A-Z

*An alphabetical list of all the Celtic boys'
names listed in this book and the chapter
in which they can be found.*

Adair ....*Roles*

Adeon ....*Personality traits*

Adhamh ....*Roles*

Adwen ....*Personality traits*

Aed...................*Personality traits*

Aedan...............*Personality traits*

Ael ....*Physical features*

Aelhaeran ....*Physical features*

Aengus ....*Physical features*

Aichear..............*Personality traits*

Aidan ....*Personality traits*

Aiden ....*Personality traits*

Ailbe..................*Physical features*

Ailbhe ....*Physical features*

Ailgenan ....*Personality traits*

Ailill..................*Physical features*

Ailin ....*Physical features*

Aindreas...........*Personality traits*

Ainéislis.............*Personality traits*

Ainmire.............................*Roles*

Airell ....*Roles*

Alain ....*Physical features*

Alan ....*Physical features*

Alasdair............................*Roles*

Alastair.............................*Roles*

Allan.................*Physical features*

Allen.................*Physical features*

Allie ....*Physical features*

Ally ....*Physical features*

Alroy.................*Physical features*

Alun ....*Physical features*

Alusdar.............................*Roles*

Anarawad ....*Physical features*

Aneurin.............*Personality traits*

Anghus ....*Physical features*

Angus ....*Physical features*

Angwyn ....*Physical features*

Annan ....*Places*

Aodh ....*Personality traits*

Aodhan ....*Personality traits*

Aodhgagan ....*Personality traits*

Arc'hantael ......*Personality traits*

Ardal ....*Personality traits*

Ardan ....*Personality traits*

Argyle..............................*Places*

Argyll...............................*Places*

Arlan ....*Personality traits*

Arlen ....*Personality traits*

Arlin ....*Personality traits*

Arlyn ....*Personality traits*

Armanz ....*Roles*

Art ....*Personality traits*

Artair ....*Personality traits*

Arte ....*Personality traits*

Arthfael	*Personality traits*	Baruch	*Personality traits*
Arthur	*Personality traits*	Bastian	*Places*
Arthur	*Personality traits*	Baudwin	*Personality traits*
Artie	*Personality traits*	Beacan	*Physical features*
Artis	*Personality traits*	Bearach	*Roles*
Arto	*Personality traits*	Beathan	*Personality traits*
Arty	*Personality traits*	Becan	*Physical features*
Arzhel	*Personality traits*	Bedivere	*Personality traits*
Arzhur	*Personality traits*	Bedwyr	*Personality traits*
Athol	*Places*	Beineon	*Personality traits*
Auley	*Roles*	Bernard	*Personality traits*
Auryn	*Physical features*	Bernez	*Personality traits*
Baird	*Roles*	Berwin	*Personality traits*
Balfour	*Places*	Bevan	*Roles*
Balor	*Personality traits*	Bevyn	*Roles*
Banadel	*Places*	Bladud	*Personality traits*
Banier	*Roles*	Blaez	*Personality traits*
Banning	*Physical features*	Blaine	*Physical features*
Bard	*Roles*	Blainey	*Physical features*
Barden	*Roles*	Blair	*Places*
Bardon	*Roles*	Blane	*Physical features*
Barnaby	*Roles*	Blayne	*Physical features*
Barnaib	*Roles*	Blayney	*Physical features*
Barra	*Roles*	Boden	*Physical features*
Barris	*Roles*	Bodie	*Physical features*
Barry	*Roles*	Body	*Physical features*
Bartley	*Roles*	Bowden	*Physical features*

Bowdyn	*Physical features*	Brentley	*Places*
Bowen	*Roles*	Brently	*Places*
Bowie	*Physical features*	Brenton	*Places*
Bowyn	*Roles*	Bressal	*Personality traits*
Boyd	*Physical features*	Bret	*Places*
Boyden	*Physical features*	Brett	*Places*
Boynton	*Places*	Brevalaer	*Personality traits*
Bradan	*Events*	Briac	*Personality traits*
Bran	*Physical features*	Briag	*Personality traits*
Brandan	*Physical features*	Briagenn	*Personality traits*
Brandubh	*Physical features*	Brian	*Personality traits*
Brann	*Physical features*	Briano	*Personality traits*
Brannoc	*Physical features*	Briant	*Personality traits*
Brannock	*Physical features*	Brice	*Physical features*
Branwell	*Places*	Briciu	*Physical features*
Brarn	*Physical features*	Briec	*Personality traits*
Brassal	*Personality traits*	Brien	*Personality traits*
Brastias	*Personality traits*	Brin	*Places*
Brazil	*Personality traits*	Brion	*Personality traits*
Breanainn	*Roles*	Broc	*Personality traits*
Breandan	*Roles*	Brodie	*Places*
Bredon	*Events*	Broin	*Physical features*
Brendan	*Roles*	Bryan	*Personality traits*
Brendt	*Places*	Bryant	*Personality traits*
Brennan	*Personality traits*	Bryce	*Physical features*
Brent	*Places*	Bryn	*Places*
Brenten	*Places*	Bryon	*Personality traits*

Buadhach..........*Personality traits*	Caoimhin..........*Physical features*
Buchanan .... *Places*	Campbell ....*Physical features*
Budoc...............................*Events*	Caolan..............*Physical features*
Burgess ....*Roles*	Car ....*Roles*
Cabhan .... *Places*	Caradec.............*Personality traits*
Caddell..............*Personality traits*	Caradoc ....*Personality traits*
Cadell ....*Personality traits*	Caradog ....*Personality traits*
Cadeyrn ....*Roles*	Caratacos ....*Personality traits*
Cadfael...............................*Roles*	Caratacus ....*Personality traits*
Cadman ....*Roles*	Carbry ....*Roles*
Cadwallader......................*Roles*	Cardew .... *Places*
Cael ....*Physical features*	Carew .... *Places*
Cahal.................*Physical features*	Carey................................ *Places*
Cahir ....*Physical features*	Carlin ....*Personality traits*
Cailean..............*Physical features*	Carney................................*Roles*
Cairbre ....*Roles*	Carr ....*Roles*
Calatin..............................*Events*	Carranog...........................*Roles*
Calder .... *Places*	Carrick ....*Physical features*
Caley ....*Physical features*	Cary .... *Places*
Calhoun.......................... *Places*	Casey.................*Personality traits*
Calum .... *Physical features*	Cassidy .... *Physical features*
Camden .... *Places*	Caswallan ....*Roles*
Cameron...........*Physical features*	Cathair ....*Roles*
Camey ....*Physical features*	Cathal................................*Roles*
Canank.............................*Roles*	Cathaoir ....*Roles*
Canice ....*Physical features*	Cathbad ....*Events*
Caoimhghin......*Physical features*	Cathmore...........................*Roles*

Cavan	*Places*	Conal	*Physical features*
Cearbhall	*Roles*	Conall	*Physical features*
Cearul	*Roles*	Conan	*Physical features*
Cecil	*Roles*	Conchobar	*Roles*
Cerwyn	*Personality traits*	Condan	*Places*
Chad	*Roles*	Condon	*Places*
Christie	*Roles*	Conlan	*Personality traits*
Cian	*Physical features*	Conlaoch	*Personality traits*
Ciar	*Physical features*	Conn	*Personality traits*
Ciaran	*Physical features*	Connal	*Physical features*
Cillian	*Roles*	Connall	*Physical features*
Cillín	*Roles*	Connell	*Physical features*
Clancy	*Roles*	Conroy	*Personality traits*
Clearie	*Roles*	Conway	*Personality traits*
Cleary	*Roles*	Corcoran	*Physical features*
Cledwin	*Personality traits*	Corentin	*Events*
Clooney	*Places*	Corey	*Places*
Cluny	*Places*	Cormac	*Roles*
Clyde	*Places*	Cormack	*Roles*
Coilin	*Roles*	Cormick	*Roles*
Coinneach	*Physical features*	Cradawg	*Personality traits*
Colla	*Roles*	Cradock	*Personality traits*
Colm	*Personality traits*	Craig	*Places*
Colman	*Personality traits*	Cronan	*Physical features*
Comhghall	*Roles*	Cronin	*Physical features*
Con	*Personality traits*	Cuchulainn	*Places*
Conaire	*Roles*	Cuinn	*Personality traits*

Culann ....*Roles*	Deimhne ....*Roles*
Cullan .... *Physical features*	Deiniol .... *Physical features*
Cullen .... *Physical features*	Delaney ....*Roles*
Curran ....*Roles*	Dempsey ....*Personality traits*
Dabhaidh ....*Personality traits*	Deniel .... *Physical features*
Dacey.............................. *Places*	Denzel.............................. *Places*
Dagda............................*Roles*	Dermot ....*Personality traits*
Dai....................*Personality traits*	Derry .... *Physical features*
Daibheid ....*Personality traits*	Desmond .... *Places*
Daibhi ....*Personality traits*	Devi ....*Personality traits*
Daire .... *Physical features*	Devin...............................*Roles*
Daithi .... *Physical features*	Dewain .... *Physical features*
Dalaigh.............................*Roles*	Diarmaid...........*Personality traits*
Daley ....*Roles*	Diarmuid ....*Personality traits*
Dallas .... *Places*	Dillon .... *Physical features*
Daly ....*Roles*	Diwrnach ....*Personality traits*
Dalziel .... *Places*	Domhnal.......................*Roles*
Damán .... *Physical features*	Donagh .... *Physical features*
Damhán .... *Physical features*	Donal ....*Roles*
Daragh .... *Physical features*	Donald ....*Roles*
Darby.................*Personality traits*	Donall ....*Roles*
Darcey .... *Physical features*	Donn .... *Physical features*
Darcy................. *Physical features*	Donncha .... *Physical features*
Daren .... *Physical features*	Donnelly ....*Personality traits*
Darragh.............. *Physical features*	Donovan .... *Physical features*
Davin................. *Physical features*	Doran................................*Roles*
Deaglan.............*Personality traits*	Dougal .... *Physical features*

Dougan .... *Physical features*	Éanna .... *Personality traits*
Doughal .... *Physical features*	Éber .... *Personality traits*
Douglas .... *Places*	Edan .... *Personality traits*
Doyle .... *Physical features*	Edryd .... *Roles*
Driscol .... *Roles*	Egan .... *Personality traits*
Driscoll .... *Roles*	Eibhear .... *Roles*
Driskell .... *Roles*	Eideard .... *Roles*
Drust .... *Events*	Einion .... *Roles*
Drustan .... *Events*	Eirnin .... *Physical features*
Duane .... *Physical features*	Elgin .... *Personality traits*
Dubhlainn .... *Physical features*	Elidr .... *Personality traits*
Duff .... *Physical features*	Elisud .... *Personality traits*
Duffey .... *Physical features*	Ellis .... *Personality traits*
Duffy .... *Physical features*	Elphin .... *Personality traits*
Dugald .... *Physical features*	Elwin .... *Personality traits*
Dugan .... *Physical features*	Emlyn .... *Roles*
Dughall .... *Physical features*	Emmet .... *Events*
Duncan .... *Physical features*	Emrys .... *Physical features*
Duncan .... *Physical features*	Enda .... *Personality traits*
Dunmore .... *Places*	Ennis .... *Places*
Dunstan .... *Physical features*	Eochaidh .... *Roles*
Dwayne .... *Physical features*	Eoghan .... *Personality traits*
Dylan .... *Physical features*	Eoin .... *Personality traits*
Ea .... *Physical features*	Ernan .... *Physical features*
Eachann .... *Roles*	Erskine .... *Places*
Eamon .... *Roles*	Erwan .... *Personality traits*
Eamonn .... *Roles*	Esras .... *Personality traits*

Euan .... *Personality traits*

Eurwyn .... *Physical features*

Evan .... *Personality traits*

Ewan .... *Personality traits*

Fachtna .... *Personality traits*

Faolan .... *Personality traits*

Farquhar .... *Personality traits*

Farrel .... *Personality traits*

Fearghal .... *Personality traits*

Fearghus .... *Physical features*

Feidhelm........... *Personality traits*

Féidhlimidh ...... *Personality traits*

Felan .... *Personality traits*

Felim .... *Personality traits*

Ferdia................ *Roles*

Fergal .... *Personality traits*

Fergus .... *Physical features*

Ferris .... *Physical features*

Fiachna .... *Physical features*

Fiachra .... *Physical features*

Finan................ *Physical features*

Finbar............... *Physical features*

Findlay .... *Physical features*

Finlay................ *Physical features*

Finn.................. *Physical features*

Finnbar .... *Physical features*

Finnian............. *Physical features*

Fintan................ *Physical features*

Fionn................. *Physical features*

Fiontan.............. *Physical features*

Flann................. *Physical features*

Floyd .... *Physical features*

Flynn .... *Physical features*

Fransez............................ *Places*

Gabhan .... *Physical features*

Gallagher ....*Roles*

Galvin................ *Physical features*

Gannon............. *Physical features*

Gareth .... *Personality traits*

Garvey ....*Events*

Gavin................ *Personality traits*

Gawain .... *Personality traits*

Gearoid ....*Roles*

Geraint.............. *Personality traits*

Gerwyn.............. *Personality traits*

Gethin .... *Physical features*

Gilchrist ....*Roles*

Gilmore ....*Roles*

Gilroy .... *Physical features*

Glen .... *Places*

Glendan .... *Places*

Glendon........................... *Places*

Glyn .... *Places*

Glyndwr .... *Places*

Glynn	*Places*	Innis	*Places*
Glynne	*Places*	Iollan	*Roles*
Gordon	*Places*	Iomhair	*Roles*
Govran	*Roles*	Irvin	*Places*
Grady	*Personality traits*	Irving	*Places*
Griffith	*Roles*	Irvyn	*Places*
Guthrie	*Places*	Ith	*Personality traits*
Gwencalon	*Personality traits*	Ithel	*Personality traits*
Gwenvael	*Roles*	Jago	*Roles*
Gwyn	*Physical features*	Jarlath	*Roles*
Gwynfor	*Physical features*	Joyce	*Roles*
Haco	*Personality traits*	Judoc	*Roles*
Hagen	*Roles*	Kado	*Events*
Harvey	*Personality traits*	Kai	*Places*
Heddwyn	*Personality traits*	Kane	*Events*
Helori	*Personality traits*	Kavan	*Physical features*
Herne	*Roles*	Keaghan	*Roles*
Hoel	*Personality traits*	Keane	*Physical features*
Hogan	*Personality traits*	Kearney	*Personality traits*
Hugh	*Personality traits*	Keary	*Roles*
Hurley	*Places*	Keegan	*Roles*
Hywel	*Personality traits*	Keelan	*Physical features*
Iarlaith	*Roles*	Keir	*Physical features*
Ifor	*Roles*	Keith	*Places*
Illtud	*Roles*	Kelvin	*Places*
Innes	*Places*	Kendall	*Places*
Inness	*Places*	Kendrick	*Places*

Kenneth .... *Physical features*

Kent .... *Places*

Kermit .... *Roles*

Kerry .... *Roles*

Kerwin .... *Physical features*

Kevan .... *Personality traits*

Kevin .... *Personality traits*

Kieran .... *Physical features*

Kieron .... *Physical features*

Killian................................. *Roles*

Kirwin .... *Physical features*

Labhras .... *Physical features*

Lachlan .... *Places*

Lachtna .... *Physical features*

Laoghaire .... *Roles*

Lee .... *Places*

Leigh .... *Places*

Leith .... *Places*

Lennán .... *Roles*

Lesley .... *Places*

Leslie .... *Places*

Liam .... *Personality traits*

Lincoln .... *Places*

Lir .... *Places*

Lleufer .... *Physical features*

Llew.................. *Personality traits*

Llewellyn........... *Personality traits*

Lloyd .... *Physical features*

Llyr .... *Places*

Lochlan............................ *Places*

Logan .... *Places*

Lorcan............... *Personality traits*

Lugh................. *Physical features*

Lughaidh .... *Personality traits*

Mabon .... *Roles*

Mac .... *Roles*

Maddox .... *Personality traits*

Madeg .... *Personality traits*

Mael .... *Roles*

Maeldun............................. *Roles*

Mainchin .... *Roles*

Malachy............................. *Roles*

Malcolm .... *Roles*

Manus .... *Personality traits*

Maoliosa............................ *Roles*

Marrec .... *Roles*

Marvin .... *Personality traits*

Meilyr .... *Roles*

Menguy .... *Personality traits*

Merlin .... *Places*

Mervin............... *Personality traits*

Mervyn .... *Personality traits*

Midhir .... *Roles*

Moffat .... *Places*

Molan	*Roles*	Neese	*Personality traits*
Moray	*Places*	Neil	*Roles*
Morcant	*Places*	Neill	*Roles*
Morfran	*Personality traits*	Nell	*Roles*
Morgan	*Places*	Nels	*Roles*
Morvan	*Places*	Nelson	*Roles*
Morven	*Places*	Newlin	*Places*
Morvyn	*Personality traits*	Newlyn	*Places*
Moryn	*Places*	Niall	*Roles*
Muircheartach	*Roles*	Niallan	*Roles*
Muireadach	*Roles*	Nikolaz	*Events*
Mungo	*Personality traits*	Ninian	*Personality traits*
Murdo	*Roles*	Nodhlag	*Events*
Murdoch	*Roles*	Nolan	*Roles*
Murdock	*Roles*	Nollaig	*Events*
Murray	*Places*	Nuada	*Roles*
Murtagh	*Roles*	Nye	*Personality traits*
Nairn	*Places*	Nyle	*Roles*
Naoise	*Personality traits*	Odhran	*Physical features*
Naoise	*Personality traits*	Oengus	*Physical features*
Neacal	*Events*	Oileabhear	*Places*
Neal	*Roles*	Oisin	*Physical features*
Neale	*Roles*	Olier	*Places*
Neall	*Roles*	Onilwyn	*Places*
Nealon	*Roles*	Oran	*Physical features*
Nechtan	*Personality traits*	Orin	*Physical features*
Nedeleg	*Events*	Oscar	*Roles*

Oskar ....*Roles*	Proinsias...........................*Places*
Owain................................*Roles*	Pryderi ....*Roles*
Owen ....*Personality traits*	Pwyll ....*Personality traits*
Padarn...............*Personality traits*	Quilan ....*Physical features*
Paddy ....*Roles*	Quin ....*Personality traits*
Padraic..............................*Roles*	Quinlan, , ...*Physical features*
Padraig..............................*Roles*	Quinlivan ....*Physical features*
Padrig ....*Roles*	Quinn...............*Personality traits*
Padruig ....*Roles*	Rafferty ....*Personality traits*
Paol ....*Personality traits*	Raghallaigh.......*Personality traits*
Parthalan ....*Roles*	Raibeart ....*Personality traits*
Peadair..............*Physical features*	Rainbeart ....*Personality traits*
Pearce ....*Physical features*	Ramsey...........................*Places*
Pearse................*Physical features*	Randal...............*Physical features*
Pedair...............*Physical features*	Reagan ....*Personality traits*
Pedr...................*Physical features*	Reaghan ....*Personality traits*
Penwyn..............*Physical features*	Reamann ....*Roles*
Per ....*Physical features*	Reamon ....*Roles*
Peredur............................*Events*	Redmond...........................*Roles*
Pert ....*Places*	Regan ....*Personality traits*
Perth ....*Places*	Reilly, Riley ....*Personality traits*
Petroc...............*Physical features*	Rhain ....*Roles*
Phelan ....*Personality traits*	Rhodri...............................*Roles*
Phelim..............*Personality traits*	Rhydderch ....*Physical features*
Piran ....*Personality traits*	Rhydwyn ....*Places*
Pol.....................*Personality traits*	Riagán ....*Personality traits*
Powell...............................*Roles*	Rian..................................*Roles*

49

Riobard	*Personality traits*	Seosamh	*Personality traits*
Riordan	*Roles*	Setanta	*Personality traits*
Roarke	*Roles*	Seumas	*Roles*
Roddy	*Places*	Shane	*Roles*
Rogan	*Physical features*	Shanley	*Physical features*
Roibeard	*Personality traits*	Shaun	*Roles*
Roibeart	*Personality traits*	Shawn	*Roles*
Ronan	*Personality traits*	Shea	*Personality traits*
Rooney	*Physical features*	Sheridan	*Roles*
Rory	*Roles*	Sinclair	*Places*
Ross	*Places*	Siridean	*Roles*
Rowan	*Physical features*	Sloan	*Roles*
Roy	*Physical features*	Sloane	*Roles*
Rúadhán	*Physical features*	Somerlad	*Roles*
Ruairí	*Physical features*	Somerled	*Roles*
Ruairidh	*Roles*	Somhairle	*Roles*
Ruari	*Roles*	Sorley	*Roles*
Ryan	*Roles*	Suibhne	*Personality traits*
Samzun	*Personality traits*	Sullivan	*Physical features*
Sawyer	*Roles*	Tadg	*Roles*
Scanlan	*Roles*	Tadhg	*Roles*
Scanlon	*Roles*	Taliesin	*Physical features*
Scott	*Places*	Tanet	*Personality traits*
Seaghdh	*Physical features*	Tangi	*Personality traits*
Seamus	*Roles*	Tanguy	*Personality traits*
Sean	*Roles*	Taran	*Personality traits*
Semias	*Roles*	Teaghue	*Roles*

Teague	*Roles*	Tudual	*Roles*
Tearlach	*Physical features*	Tully	*Roles*
Tiarnán	*Roles*	Turlach	*Physical features*
Tiernan	*Roles*	Turloch	*Physical features*
Tierney	*Roles*	Turlough	*Physical features*
Tomas	*Physical features*	Uaine	*Places*
Torin	*Roles*	Uilliam	*Personality traits*
Torrance	*Places*	Uinseann	*Personality traits*
Torrey	*Places*	Ultan	*Roles*
Tory	*Places*	Urien	*Roles*
Trahern	*Physical features*	Varden	*Places*
Trefor	*Places*	Vardon	*Places*
Tremaine	*Places*	Vaughan	*Physical features*
Tremayne	*Places*	Vaughn	*Physical features*
Trevor	*Places*	Visant	*Personality traits*
Tris	*Events*	Vychan	*Personality traits*
Tristan	*Events*	Waylon	*Places*
Tristen	*Events*	Weylyn	*Personality traits*
Tristian	*Events*	Wynford	*Physical features*
Tristin	*Events*	Wynne	*Physical features*
Tristram	*Events*	Yann	*Personality traits*
Tuathal	*Roles*	Yestin	*Personality traits*
Tudor	*Roles*		

GIRLS'
NAMES

INTRODUCTION

In this chapter you will find over 650 Celtic girls' names, from Aamor, meaning warmth and affection, to Zinerva, meaning white wave or tribeswoman. These girls' names are either of Celtic origin or have been widely adopted amongst Celtic peoples. A name like Shauna, for example, which is a derivation form of the biblical name John, is included because, while not necessarily having Celtic origins, it is a name used by the Celts.

The section is broken down into chapters, so that the names are categorized under Events, Personality Traits, Physical Features, Place Names and Roles. For example, a name like Bronte, meaning generous, will be listed under Personality Traits, while a name like Aibrean, the Gaelic for April, comes under Events.

EVENTS

The names in this section relate to events and happenings, both specific events, such as a famous battle or a legend, and generic occurrences such as victory.

Aibrean
(Ab-rawn)
Gaelic for April.
Aibrean can also be spelt
Aibreann.

Aibreann
(Ab-rawn)
April.

Athract
(A-trocht)
A great change.

Coinchend
(Ko-in-hend)
Pledge or covenant.

Hayley
(Hay-lee)
Meaning escape, originally the
name of a town, derived from
the Old English words 'heg' for
hay and 'leah' for clearing.

Nodhlaig
(Null-ig)
Birthday. Nodhlaig is a name
of French and Latin origins,
derived from the name Noelle
and boys' name Noel, meaning
Christmas.

Nollaig
(No-lag)
Birthday. See Nodhlaig.

Personality Traits

The names in this section all have meanings that could describe a person's character. Meanings range from elements, such as fire, to animals, such as hounds or birds, and names in honour of gods and heroes, all of which bestow certain attributes upon the person bearing that name.

Aamor
(Ah-mor)
Similar to the French word for love, 'aamor' is Celtic for warmth and affection.

Aednat
(Ay-nit)
Often Anglicized to Ena, Aednat is the feminine form of Aidan, and means spark or little fire.

Aela
(Ay-la)
A Breton name associated with strength, either in the sense of love (ardour) or in physical objects, such as rocks and ramparts.

Affraic
(Aff-ric)
A name that originated in Ireland, meaning agreeable or pleasant. Other forms of Affraic are Aifric, Afric and Africa, the latter being an Anglicized form.

Afric
(Aff-ric)
Pleasant. See variant Affraic.

Africa
(Aff-ric-ah)
Pleasant. See variant Affraic.

Aideen
(Ay-deen)
Fire. Derived from the word 'aed', meaning fire, Aideen was the name of a legendary Irish heroine.

THE LEGEND OF AIDEEN

In Irish folklore, Aideen is the wife of Oscar, son of Oisin and the fairy Niamh, and grandson of Fionn Mac Cumhail. Oisín is a brave warrior who slays three kings, but falls at the Battle of Gabhra. Hearing of her loss, Aideen dies of a broken heart and is buried in a tomb, now situated in Howth Castle near Dublin, which is covered by a huge capstone. The tomb of Aideen can still be seen today.

Aigneis

(Ag-nees)
A Celtic form of the Greek name Agnes, meaning holy and pure.

Ailbe

(Al-beh or Al-veh)
White, in the sense of purity. Ailbe is a name used for boys and girls. In Irish legend, Ailbe was the daughter of Midir, the fairy king, and St Ailbe was a 6th-century monk from Co Tipperary, who blessed a barren river and made it abundant with fish. Churches were built in his honour at the five best fishing places along the river.

Aileen

(Ay-leen)
Little noble one. Aileen is derived from the word 'ail', meaning noble.

Ailene

(Ay-leen)
Little noble one. See Aileen.

ĀINE: THE FAIRY QUEEN

Aine is the queen of the Munster fairies and is revered in Irish folklore as a goddess of love, a protector of women, crops and livestock, and a bringer of fruitfulness and prosperity. She is said to have been ravaged by the king of Munster, but exacts her revenge by biting off his ear, thus rendering him unfit to rule. Legend has it that she created a magical fairy race and is still honoured at the Summer Solstice with torchlit processions.

Ailidh
(Ay-lay)
A variant form of the Scottish name Eilidh, meaning kind.

Ailis
(Ay-lish)
God is my oath. Ailis is derived from the French Alice, a form of Elizabeth, which means God is my oath.
Ailis can also be spelt Ailish, Eilis or Eilish.

Ailish
(Ay-lish)
God is my oath. See Ailis.

Aina
(Awn-ya)
Radiant joy. See Aine.

Aine
(Awn-ya)
Derived from the Irish word for splendour or brilliance, the name Aine means brilliant or radiant joy and is associated

with prosperity.
Aine can be Anglicized as Anya,
Anna or Hannah.

Aineislis
(An-ash-lis)
Careful and thoughtful.

Aingeal
(An-gil)
Angel.

Airic
(Ay-ric)
Agreeable.

Aithne
(Ay-ne)
Fire. A feminine form of Aidan.

Alana
(A-lah-na)
A feminine form of Alan, or
derived from Ailin, meaning little
rock, Alana can mean harmony,
stone, noble or fair. In other
cases it is derived from the word
'leanbh' meaning child, the 'a'
giving a sense of fondness, hence
beloved child or darling child.

Alane
(A-lan)
Fair.

Alanna
(A-la-na)
Harmony, stone, noble, fair, or
beloved child. See Alana.

Alannah
(A-la-na)
Harmony, stone, noble, fair, or
beloved child. See Alana.

Aleine
(Ar-lane)
Can mean precious or sunbeam.

Alice
(A-liss)
Noble, exalted.

Alma
(Al-ma)
A popular name in Latinate
languages, in Celtic Alma means
good.

Almha
(Alm-ha)
An alternative name for the

ANDRASTE: THE WARRIOR GODDESS

When Boudicca, queen of the Celtic Iceni tribe, rallied her troops for her campaign against the Romans, she is said to have called upon the favour of Andraste, the warrior goddess, who was believed to bestow courage in the face of battle. After Boudicca sacked London, the Roman women were taken to a place dedicated to the worship of Andraste and brutally slaughtered and mutilated. The spot, believed to be in what is now Epping Forest, north of London, was known as Andraste's Grove.

goddess Almu, who gave her name to a hill in Leinster.

Alys
(A-liss)
Noble. A variant of Alice.

Amena (A-mee-na)
Possibly derived from the Arabic name Amina, meaning honesty, Amena means absolutely pure or honest.

Anchoret
(An-kraht)
An Anglicized variant of the Welsh name Angharad, meaning greatly loved.

Andraste
(An-dras-tay)
Invincible.
Andraste was a goddess revered by the Iceni tribe of southern England.

Aneira
(An-ay-ra)
Honourable or honoured. From
the Welsh 'eira', meaning snow,
Aneira is associated with
moral purity.

Angharad
(An-ha-rad)
A Welsh name meaning greatly
loved. The name Angharad has
been in use for at least 1,200
years and was a character in
the Mabinogion, a collection of
Welsh folk tales compiled in the
12th century.

Annaic
(A-nah-eek)
A Breton name meaning
favoured by God, Annaic is a
variant of Anne. According to
Breton legend, St Anne, mother
of the Virgin Mary, was born in
Brittany, and she is the patron
saint of the region.

Annaig
(A-nah-eek)
Favoured by God. See Annaic.

Annick
(An-eek)
Favoured by God. See Annaic.

Annowre
(An-our-ri)
Honourable or honoured.
A variant of Aneira.

Aphria
(A-free-ah)
Agreeable.

Ardanata
(Ar-dan-ar-ta)
Exalted or honoured. A name
from Welsh legend.

Arden
(Ar-den)
Eager or ardent.

Ardena
(Ar-dee-na)
Eager or ardent.

Ardene
(Ar-deen)
Eager or ardent.

Ardra

(Ar-dra)
Noble.

Argante

(Ar-gan-ti)
In Arthurian legend, Argante, known as the silver queen, was the goddess of the underworld, to whom Arthur was taken to cure him of his mortal wounds.

Arienh

(Ar-een)
A promise, pledge or oath.

Arlana

(Ar-lahn-a)
A promise, pledge or oath.
A variant of Arienh.

Arleen

(Ar-leen)
A promise, pledge or oath.
A variant of Arienh.

Arlene

(Ar-leen)
A promise, pledge or oath.
A variant of Arienh.

Arleta

(Ar-leta)
A promise, pledge or oath.
A variant of Arienh.

Arlette

(Ar-let)
A promise, pledge or oath.
A variant of Arienh.

Arlina

(Ar-leen-a)
A promise, pledge or oath.
A variant of Arienh.

Arline

(Ar-leen)
A promise, pledge or oath.
A variant of Arienh.

Armelle

(Ar-may)
A Breton name, Armelle is the feminine form of Armel, which is derived from the words 'art', meaning stone or bear, and 'mael', which means chief, prince or disciple.

THE LEGEND OF AZENOR

In Breton folklore, Azenor is the only child of Even, Lord of Brest. She is the victim of her stepmother's jealousy and falsely accused of adultery. Her punishment is to be set adrift at sea in a barrel, where she is visited by an angel, who keeps her alive for five months until she reaches the shore of Ireland. Pregnant with her husband's child, she gives birth to Budoc, later Saint Budoc, who returns to the Breton nobility after Azenor's death.

Azenor

(Ah-zay-nor)
A name of Breton origin that means sunray or shining light. It is a variant of Elinor.

Beatha

(Ba-ha)
Life.

Becuma

(Bec-yu-mah)
Becuma is a character from Irish mythology and the name means lonely woman.

Berched

(Bair-xed)
Heavenly or exalted. A Breton variant of the Irish Brighid.

Betha

(Bay-thah)
Life. A variant of Beatha.

Bethan

(Be-than)
Life. A variant of Beatha.

Breched

(Bray-xed)
Heavenly. See Berched.

Breed

(Breed)

Strong and powerful. Breed is a variant of Brid and Bridget.

Breeda

(Bree-da)

Strong and powerful.
See Breed.

Briaca

(Bree-ah-kah)

Female version of Briac, thought to be the origin of Brian. Maybe derived from the French name Briaga. The origin is uncertain, possibly the female version of Breck, meaning freckled.

Briana

(Bree-a-na)

Virtuous, noble and strong. The female version of Brian.

Briann

(Bree-an)

Virtuous, noble and strong. See Briana.

Brianna

(Bree-a-na)

Virtuous, noble and strong.
See Briana.

Briannah

(Bree-an)

Virtuous, noble and strong.
See Briana.

Brianne

(Bree-an)

Virtuous, noble and strong.
See Briana.

Briannon

(Bree-an)

Virtuous, noble and strong.
See Briana.

Brid

(Breed)

Strong and powerful. A popular Irish variant of Bridget. See Breed.

Bride

(Bride)

Strong and powerful. Once a popular name in England and Scotland, but now rare. See Breed.

Bridget
(Bri-jit)
Strong and powerful. A popular variant of Brighid and name of the Celtic goddess of wisdom. Other variants include Biddy, Dina and Delia. See Breed.

Bridie
(Bry-dee)
Esteemed and strong. See Bride and Bridget.

Brienna
(Bree-en-a)
Virtuous, noble and strong. See Briana.

Brienne
(Bree-en)
Virtuous, noble and strong. See Briana.

Brietta
(Bree-et-ta)
Strong and esteemed. As a variant of the English name Briar, it can mean thorny wild roses. See Breed and Bridget.

Brighid
(Breed)
Strong and powerful. See Breed and Bridget.

Brigid
(Bri-jid)
Strong and powerful. Irish goddess of fire. See Breed and Bridget.

Brigitta
(Bri-jee-ta)
Strong and esteemed. Thought to have German origins and also to be the name of a Russian monk. See Bridget.

Brigitte
(Bri-jeet)
Strong. French variant, see Bridget.

Brite
(Breet)
Strong. See Bret and Bridget.

Brites
(Bree-tesh)
Strong and exalted one. See Bret and Bridget.

THE POWER OF BRIGID

The name Brigid is derived from the word 'brigh', meaning power, vigour and virtue, and is found throughout Irish history and legend. Goddess Brigid is behind the fruitful land and animals, and also a patron of poets and blacksmiths. Along with St Patrick and St Columba in helpings of Irish esteem, St Brigid of Kildare appeared in the Christian era, with stories of her compassion and miracles still told all over Ireland today after 1,500 years. Her feast day is 1 February, the first day of spring in the Celtic calendar.

Britta
(Brit-a)
Strong and exalted one. See Bret and Bridget.

Brona
(Bro-nah)
Sad. Brona is a Gaelic name thought to be a variant of Bronagh, meaning sorrowful.

Bronagh
(Bro-nah)
Derived from the word 'bronach' meaning sad. St Bronagh was a 6th-century mystic.

Bronte
(Bron-tee)
Generous. Bronte is derived from the Gaelic word 'proinnteach', meaning bestower.

Bryana
(Bry-anna)
Strong and noble, also a hill.
A female variant of Brian. See
Briana.

Bryann
(Bry-a-na)
Strong and noble. See Briana.

Bryanna
(Bry-an-na)
Strong and noble. See Briana.

Bryanne
(Bry-anne)
Strong and noble. See Briana.

Brygid
(Bree-jid)
Strong and powerful. See
Bridget.

Caitlin
(Kate-lin or Koit-leen)
Pure and courageous. This Gaelic
variant of Cathleen derives from
the old French Cateline and
Catherine, and is associated with
Greek origins.

Caitriona
(Kat-ree-o-na)
Pure. A popular name in Ireland
and Scotland. See Caitlin.

Carey
(Keh-ree)
From the word 'caru' for love,
Carey's Welsh roots, meaning hill
fort, come from Carew Castle,
while its Irish meaning derives
from the name Ciardha, meaning
black and also a descendant of the
dark one.

Caronwyn
(Kar-on-win)
Pure and loved. A variant of
Caronwen.

Cary
(Keh-ree)
From the fortress. See Carey.

Catriona
(Ka-tree-ona)
Pure. A Gaelic form of
Catherine, found mostly in
Irish and Scottish names. See
Caitlin.

THE GREAT FLOOD AND THE FIRST IRISH SETTLERS

Irish legend has it that Cessair was Noah's grand-daughter, but despite this family tie, Noah didn't allow her aboard the ark. So, advised by an idol she had her father build, she took fifty women and three men by ship on a seven-year journey to become the first settlers in Ireland, landing at Bantry Bay, a poignant forty days before the Great Flood. Turning into a salmon, Fintan was the only flood survivor.

Ceasg
(Kask)
Dark and sorrowful.

Ceinlys
(Kane-liss)
Beautiful and sweet, from Welsh origins, also possibly associated with wealth.

Ceri
(Keh-ree)
Blessed poetry. Ceri is also thought to come from the Welsh word 'caru', meaning love. The village of Porth Ceri is in the Vale of Glamorgan and Ceri is also the name of a river in Ceredigion. Ceri be a boys' name too. See Ceridwen.

Cessair
(Kess-air)
Great sorrow. A variant of Ceasair. Cessair was married to Úgaine Mor, High King of Ireland around the 6th century.

Cobhlaith
(Kov-lah)

SHAKESPEARE'S CORDELIA

A rarely found woman of virtue and heart, Cordelia was the unfortunate victim of her father King Lear, who promised her a third of his kingdom, in return for her undying love for him.

> *Unhappy that I am, I cannot heave*
> *My heart into my mouth. I love your majesty*
> *According to my bond; no more nor less.*

Unlike her obliging, deceitful sisters, her refusal results in her banishment from the land.

Victorious. Very old Irish name, of uncertain origin, first recorded around the 7th century as a variant of Choblaith.

Cordelia
(Kor-deel-ya)
Jewel of the sea. Cordelia is derived from Welsh legend Creiddylad.

Creiddylad
(Kred-il-ad)
Jewel of the sea. Also associated with the Welsh word 'creyr', meaning heron. Creiddylad is associated with the name Cordelia.

Creidne
(Kredge-ni)
Honour and faith. A Fianna warrior from Irish and Scottish mythology, from a band of mercenaries often used by kings in wartime. Not linked to Creidhne the builder god.

Creirwy
(Krer-we)
A Welsh name meaning jewel.

Crisiant
(Kris-ee-ent)
Welsh name and a variant of the
English Crystal.

Cruatha
(Krew-a-ha)
Firm or solid.

Crystal
(Kris-tal)
Meaning is uncertain but the name
is associated with the Greek for ice.

Cyhyreath
(Koo-hoo-reth)
Weeping or great sadness.

Dacie
(Da-see)
Clear and pure, from the
south. An Irish Gaelic variant
of the English Dacey and Latin
Candace.

CREIDDYLAD AND AFFAIRS OF THE HEART

Creiddylad was betrothed to one lover and abducted by another, leading to King Arthur ordering a duel between her two lovers each May Day till Doomsday. Meanwhile, poor Creiddylad had to stay with her father, Lludd of the Silver Hand and ruler of plague-ridden Britain. A similar tale is told where she is the daughter of Llyr, god of the sea, and the object of desire between gods Gwyn and Gwyrthur. The goddess of summer flowers, she is also known as the May Queen and is celebrated in many Celtic covens.

Daimhin
(Daw-veen)
Little deer. Daimhin is a variant of Davin and Davina. This can also be a boy's name.

Dee
(Dee)
Swarthy and dark. A name of Welsh origin.

Deheune
(Deh-voon)
Divine one. A variant of Devin.

Deniela
(Day-nee-ella)
God has judged. Deniela is a female version of the boys' name Deniel, derived from the biblical Daniel.

Derryth
(Der-rith)
Of the oak.

Deva
(Dee-vah)
Divine one. A Celtic name that may be traced back to Hindi origins.

Devona
(Deh-voh-na)
Divine one. A variant of the old English Devon, the name of a county in England's Celtic West Country.

Dilic
(Dill-iss)
Genuine, true. A variant of Dilys.

Dilys
(Dill-iss)
A Welsh name meaning genuine, true.

Dindrane
(Din-drain)
Immaculate. Dindrane was the sister of Percival in Arthurian legend and a heroine, though often unnamed, in stories of the Holy Grail.

Diorbhail
(Dee-or-ba)
Gift of God. Diorbhail is a Gaelic variant of the Scottish Dorothy.

Diva
(Dee-va)
Divine one. See Deva.

Divone
(Di-vone)
Divine one. See Deva.

Dogmaela
(Dog-may-la)
Sharing. Dogmaela is derived
from the Welsh for apportion.

Doireann
(Dor-ree-an)
Brooding. An Irish name
Anglicized as Doreen.

Doreen
(Dore-een)
Brooding. Doreen is an
Anglicized form of Doireann.

Doreena
(Dore-ee-na)
Brooding. See Doreen.

Drusilla
(Droo-sill-a)
Strong. Drusilla is a Gaelic name
derived from the Roman clan
name Drusus.

Dwyn
(Dwin)
A Welsh name meaning pleasant,
holy or fair.

Dwynen
(Dwin-en)
Meaning white wave, derived
from the Welsh words 'dwyn'
and 'gwen'. St Dwynen is the
Welsh version of St Valentine,
celebrated on 25th January.

Dymphna
(Dimf-na)
Fawn, but also associated with
poetry and being fit and suitable.
Also spelt Dympna and Dimpna.

Eabha
(Ay-va)
Breath of life. Eabha was a wife
of Nemed, the legendary invader
of Ireland.

Eachna
(Ack-na)
Steed, horse. Eachna was the
beautiful and clever daughter
of the Irish king of Connacht,
revered for her looks and style.

SAINT DYMPHNA

An Irish virgin, Dymphna escaped the incestuous clutches of her father, King Damon, who fixated on his daughter becoming her dead mother's successor as she bore an uncanny resemblance to her. When Damon found his daughter in Belgium, she refused to marry him, so he chopped off her head. She became a patron saint of those affected by mental illness, incest and insanity.

Eadain
(Ay-deen)
Jealousy. Eadain is a modern variant of Etaín.

Eadaoin
(Ay-deen)
Blessed with friends, or jealousy. See Eadain.

Ealasaid
(Eel-a-sade)
God is my oath. Ealasaid is a Scottish variant of Elizabeth.

Ealga
(Ale-ga)
Noble and brave. Ealga is used poetically to represent Ireland: 'Innis Ealga', in other words the Noble Isle.

Edana
(Eh-dah-na)
Passionate and fiery. Edana is a Latinized variant of Etaín. See Aideen.

Edna
(Ed-na)
Kernel or nut. Edna is the

Anglicized version of the Gaelic
Eithne.

Eilis

(Eye-leesh)
God is my oath. Eilis is an Irish
variant of Alice or Elizabeth. See
Ailis.

Eimhear

(Ee-mer)
Swift. See Eimear.

Eithne

(Ee-na or En-ya)
Kernel or nut. Eithne was also
the mother of St Columba.

Eitna

(En-ya)
Kernel or nut. See Eithna.

Elaine

(Ee-lane or Eh-lane)
Fawn, or sun ray, shining light.
The latter meaning is derived
from Greek origins. Elaine
appears in Arthurian legend,
where she falls for Lancelot.

Elsha

(El-sha)
Noble.

Enat

(Ay-net)
A Gaelic name meaning little fire
and the female version of Aidan.

Enda

(En-da)
Birdlike, a free spirit. Enda is
also used as a boys' name.
St Enda was a 6th-century Irish
warrior-turned-monk from the
Aran Islands.

Engl

(En-gel)
Light.

Enid

(Ee-nid)
Life and soul, with spirit.
Enid is of Welsh origin and
appears as Geraint's wife in
Arthurian legend.

Enora

(Eh-no-rah)
Breton name meaning honour.
Also from the Greek Eleanor,

Girls: *Personality Traits*

THE ENVY OF ETAIN

The most beautiful and gentle woman in the world, Etain is said to have even been jealous of herself. Fuamnach, the wife of fairy king Midir, who was in love with Etain, turned her into a puddle, a worm and a butterfly, swept by the wind over the sea for seven years till she was caught and looked after by Oengus, who was warring with Midir. Fuamnach found out and created a gust to blow her away for another seven years. On her return to Ireland, she landed in a glass of wine drunk by a woman longing for a child, and so was reborn and married High King Eochaid Airem.

meaning shining light. Variant of Honoria. St Enora and St Efflam took vows of chastity after their marriage and were together for the rest of their lives.

Enya
(En-yah)
Nut or fire. See Eithne.

Erena
(Eh-ray-na)
Bright light and peace. Erena is a variant of the Greek Irene, and Irish and English Erin and Helen.

Ertha
(Er-tha)
Strong faith or firm belief. A Cornish variant of the Old English Eartha and Hertha.

Etain
(Eh-tane)
Meaning jealousy and also linked with horses.

Eubha
(Eu-b-ha or Oob-ha)
A Scottish name, with mixed origins, mostly from the Hebrew for full of life. A variant of Eva.

Eurielle
(Yoo-ree-elle)
Thought to mean angelic, of uncertain origin.

Evelina
(Ev-eh-lee-na)
Light or bird. A Latinized version of Evelyn.

Eveline
(Eve-eh-line)
Light or bird. See Evelina.

Fainche
(Fan-ke)
Raven, freedom or wanderer. Also the name of a saint of Rossory at Lough Erne.

THE FAVOURED VARIANTS OF FEIDELM

Versions of this popular name feature heavily in Irish mythology, including as a prophetess, the 'nine times beautiful' warrior princess Feidelm Noíchrothach, also the daughter of Ulster king Conchobhar and the granddaughter of Niall of the Nine Hostages. It is also the name of six saints.

Fedelma
(Feh-del-ma)
Meaning faithful, and a variant of
Feidelm and Fidelma.

Feenat
(Fee-en-at)
Deer.

Fidelma
(Fid-el-ma)
Faithful. See Fedelma.

Firinne
(Fi-rin)
Irish name meaning truth or
fidelity.

Flaitheas
(Flaw-his)
An Irish name meaning sovereign
or royal.

Frann
(Fran)
Sea bird, or from France. Frann
can be used as an abbreviated
form of the name Frances,
meaning Frenchwoman.

Ganieda
(Gan-yay-da)
Morning star. Ganieda is thought
to relate to the morning star, a
variant of Gwendydd, Merlin's
sister in Arthurian legend.

Gearoidin
(Gar-ro-dean)
Irish name for a noble warrior.
Gearoidin is the female version
of the English boys' name
Gerald, which means ruler of the
spear, of Germanic origin.

Gilda
(Gil-da or Jill-dah)
Old English name meaning
a layer of gold. Also meaning
sacrifice.

Gildas
(Gil-das)
Sacrifice. See Gilda.

Glenda
(Glen-da)
Pure. Glenda is a Welsh name
meaning clean and good from
the words 'giân' and 'da'.

Grainne
(Graw-nya)
From the Gaelic word 'grán' for grain and also connected with love. The origin of Grania. In Irish legend, Grainne was the wife of Fionn Mac Cool and lover of Diarmuid, a pirate heroine and also an Irish grain goddess.

Grania
(Gra-nya)
Love or grain. Grania is derived from the word 'graidh' and is a Latinized variant of Grainne.

Gunoda
(Goo-noh-da)
A Cornish name of uncertain origin and meaning, thought to mean blessed.

Gwendydd
(Gwen-did)
Morning star.
Gwendydd was Merlin's sister in Arthurian legend.

Gwener
(Gwen-er)
Relating to love, this is the Welsh equivalent of Venus.

Gwyneth
(Gwin-eth)
Meaning happiness and luck, a Welsh name thought to come from the area of Gwynedd. Also fair and pure. See Gwen.

Gwynith
(Gwin-ith)
Happiness and luck or fair and pure. See Gwen and Gwyneth.

Haude
(Ode)
A Breton name meaning noble.

Helori
(Hay-loh-ree)
Generous, giving. Helori is an Old Breton name derived from the word 'hael', meaning generous.

Heodez
(Hay-oh-days)
Of uncertain meaning, Heodez was a 6th-century princess and saint of Brittany. Believing false rumours, her faithless brother Tangi ordered her decapitation. But she put her head back on and was as good as new. Tangi did penance and became a saint too.

Heulwen
(Hiel-wen or Hyool-win)
A Welsh name meaning sunshine.

Hieretha
(He-er-ee-tha)
A Cornish name meaning holy
and upright.

Idelisa
(Eye-deh-lee-sa or Id-eh-lee-sa)
A Welsh name meaning
bountiful. Possibly of Germanic
origin.

Idelle
(Eye-dell or Id-elle)
Bountiful. See Idelisa.

Inira
(In-eer-a)
A Welsh name meaning honour.

Iseabal
(Ish-bale)
God is my oath. A Scottish
variant of Elizabeth.

Janet
(Jan-et)
God is gracious. A Scottish
variant of the Hebrew Jane.

Jannet
(Jan-nayt)
God is gracious. A Breton variant
of the Hebrew Jane.

Jennifer
(Jen-i-fer)
Fair and pure. Jennifer is a
Cornish variant of the Welsh
name Gwenhwyfar, meaning
white wave. See also Guenevere.

Kacee
(Kay-see)
Alert and vigilant. A variant of
Irish name Casey.

Kaitlin
(Kate-lin)
Pure and courageous. Also spelt
Kaitlyn and Kaytlin. See Caitlin.

Kanna
(Ka-nah)
Of uncertain origin and
meaning, a Breton saint whose
feast day is 10 March.

Katell
(Kah-tell)
Pure. A Breton version of
Katherine, also spelt Katel.

Kendra
(Ken-dra)
Wise ruler or champion of the people. A Welsh name that is also the female version of Kendrick, Gaelic for son of Henry.

Kerenza
(Keh-ren-sa)
A Cornish variant of Kerensa, meaning love.

Kew
(Kyoo)
A Cornish name of uncertain origin or meaning, usually applied in honour of Saint Kew.

Kirstie
(Kers-tee)
Follower of Christ, a variant of the Scottish name Kirsty and the Latin name Christina. See Cairistiona.

Klervi
(Clare-vee)
Of uncertain origin or meaning, this is the Breton name of a 6th-century saint. A variant of Clervie.

Koulm
(Kool-em)
A Breton Celtic girls' name which means dove.

Koulmia
(Cool-mee-a)
Dove. A variant of Koulm.

Kristen
(Kris-ten)
Follower of Christ. A Breton version of Christine. See Cairistiona.
St Kristen is celebrated on 12 November.

Kyna
(Kee-na)
Intelligent or love, derived from the word 'cion' for affection.

Lara
(La-ra or Lah-rah)
Protection. Also the Breton female version of boys' name Alar.

Lavena
(Lav-ee-na)
Anglicized version of Lavinia, meaning mother of the Romans and joy.

Lena

(Lay-nah)
Sunshine, bright light. Of uncertain origin and meaning, this name is probably a variant of Helena. See Elen.

Levenez

(Lay-veh-nez)
A Breton name meaning happiness.
Saint Levenez is celebrated on 3 November.

Lileas

(Lil-ee-as)
Lily. A Scottish version of Lillian and a variant of the Latin for Lily.

Linette

(Lin-ette)
Gentle, image or songbird. Linette is of Germanic, Old French and Welsh origins. See Eluned.

Linnet

(Lin-et)
Gentle, image or songbird. See Linette.

Linnette

(Lin-ette)
Gentle, image or songbird. See Linette.

Lynet

(Lin-ette)
Gentle, image or songbird. See Linette.

Lynette

(Lin-ette)
Gentle, image or songbird. See Linette.

Lyonesse

(Lee-on-ess)
Scottish name, meaning little lion.

Mab

(Mab)
A Gaelic, Irish and Welsh name meaning joy, or from the Welsh word 'maban' meaning child. Mab was the Queen of the Fairies in *Romeo and Juliet*.

Maban

(Mab-an)
Child.

Madailein

(Ma-da-lin)
Magnificent. An Irish version of
Madeleine and the Hebrew name
Magdalena, meaning tower.

Madenn

(Mah-den)
A Breton name meaning happy-
go-lucky.

Madrun

(Mad-roon)
Of uncertain meaning, the
English name of a Cornish saint.

Maebh

(Mayv)
From the old Irish name Medb,
meaning someone who brings
great joy or intoxicates.

Maeve

(Mayv)
Bringer of great joy and
intoxicating. See Maebh.

Maire

(Mare)
The Irish version of Mary.
Originally spelt Muire, it was
used to represent Our Lady but
was so revered that it only began
to be accepted as a normal name,
spelt Maire, at end of the 15th
century, while Muire was kept for
the Blessed Mother.

Mairi

(Ma-ree)
Mary. A variant of Maire.

Maolisa

(Mail-issa)
Follower of Jesus.

Marvina

(Mar-vee-na)
Renowned friend. Marvina is the
female version of the boys' name
Marvin, meaning sea friend in
Welsh.

Mavelle

(May-vel)
An Irish name of Old French
origin, meaning songbird.

Mavie

(May-vee)
Songbird. See Mavelle.

MEDB: THE WARRIOR QUEEN

This legendary and fearless queen of Connacht appeared in the Irish epic *The Cattle Raid of Cooley*. Feeling she had met her match, she left King Conchobar Mac Nessa for Ailill, but they clashed over which of them possessed the more illustrious herd of cows. Her attempt to buy a prestigious brown bull resulted in a bloody war between the people of Connacht and Ulster.

Mavis
(May-viss)
Songbird. See Mavelle.

Mavourna
(Ma-vorna)
My little darling.

Meadhbh
(Mayv)
Irish name thought to mean bringer of great joy and happiness, also associated with a pearl. See Maebh.

Meara
(Meer-a)
Jolly, jovial.

Medb
(Mayv)
Bringer of great joy, intoxicating. See Maebh. Medb was a great warrior queen from Irish legend.

Melle
(May-lah or Mel)
Melle originates from a Breton word meaning pregnant, and is a variant of Mary which comes from the New Testament. Saint

Melle was an Irish-born saint revered in Brittany.

Merewin

(Meh-re-win)
Renowned friend. A Cornish variant of Marvina.

Merna

(Mer-na)
Affectionate and tender. A variant of the Irish and Gaelic name Myrna.

Mikaela

(Mee-kay-lah)
Who is like God.

Mirna

(Mer-nah)
Affectionate and tender.
See Merna.

Moina

(Moi-nah)
Noble and beloved. A derivation of Muadhnait, meaning little noble one. See Merna.

Moira

(Moy-ra)
Exceptional, or star of the sea.

See Maire.

Mona

(Moh-nah)
Little noble one. See Moina.

Mór

(Mor)
Irish and Scottish name meaning exceptional and great one.

Moreen

(Mor-een)
Great. See Maureen.

Morna

(Mor-na)
Irish and Scottish name meaning affectionate and spirited. An Anglicized variant of Muirne.

Moya

(Moy-a)
Exceptional. See Maire.

Moyna

(Moy-na)
Tender, mild, or little noble one. Moyna is an Irish and Scottish variant of Mona, the Anglicized version of Muadhnait, meaning little noble one. See Moina.

Muirne
(Mir-neh)
Affectionate and high-spirited.
Muirne appears in Irish
mythology as the mother of
Fionn Mac Cool.

Mwynen
(Mwee-nen)
Someone who is gentle. A name
of Welsh origin.

Myfanwy
(Mi-fan-wee)
A Welsh name meaning my lovely
little one.

Myrna
(Mur-na)
Affectionate and spirited. See
Merna and Muirne.

Naible
(Naub-la)
Beloved.

Nanna
(Na-na)
Brave. Nanna is derived from
the Old Norse word 'nenna',
meaning brave. Nanna was the
goddess of summer and flowers,
who died of a broken heart

MUIRNE OF THE BEAUTIFUL NECK

Muirne is the mother of Fionn Mac Cool, who falls in love with Conall from an opposing tribe. This angers her druid father, who has him killed. Muirne is already pregnant and when her son is born she sends him to safety in the forest to be raised by Bodhmall and Liath Luachra. He becomes the legendary hero Fionn Mac Cool.

following the death of her husband, the moon god Balder.

Nara
(Nah-ra)
Happy and content. Nara is of Old English origins, also thought to mean nearest one.

Nareen
(Na-reen)
Happy. See Nara.

Nareena
(Na-ree-na)
Happy. See Nara.

Nareene
(Na-reen)
Happy. See Nara.

Navlin
(Nav-lin)
Holy pool. Navlin is a female form of the boys' name Newlin.

Neasa
(Nes-a)
A variant of Assa, meaning gentle. Neasa appears in Irish legend as the not so gentle mother of Conchobar, the king of Ulster.

She tricks her second husband Fergus into giving her son the kingdom for a year and then he does such a good job that his people decide to keep him for good.

Nemetona
(Nem-et-ona)
A goddess of Gaul and Roman Britain of uncertain origin, thought to be the keeper of sacred places.

Nessa
(Ness-er)
Gentle. See Neasa.

Nesta
(Ness-ter)
Chaste and pure, or serious. Nesta is a Welsh name and a variant of Agnes, of Greek origin meaning chaste and pure. Also short for the Germanic name Ernesta, meaning serious.

Nevena
(Neh-vee-na)
Little saint, or holy one. Nevena is an Irish name which has a male equivalent in Nevin and Nevan.

Nevina
(Neh-vee-na)
Little saint, or holy one. See
Nevena.

Noirin
(Noh-reen)
Shining one, or woman of
honour. Noirin is an Irish variant
of Nora.

Nolwenn
(Nol-wen)
A Breton name meaning pure,
and a person from Noal in Gaul.
St Nolwenn was the daughter of
a 6th-century prince of Cornwall,
who devoted her life to God in
solitude in Vannes.

Non
(Non)
Meaning unknown. According
to legend, St Non is the mother
of St David, the patron saint of
Wales. The Chapel of St Non in
South Wales is named after her
and is the Places of David's birth.

Nora
(Nor-ah)
Shining one, or woman of
honour. Nora is a popular Irish
name with its origins in the
Greek name Eleanora, meaning
bright, shining one, and the
Latin Leonora, meaning woman
of honour.

Norah
(Nor-ah)
Shining one, or woman of
honour. See Nora.

Noreen
(Nor-een)
Shining one, or woman of
honour. See Noirin and Nora.

Nuline
(Noo-leen)
Daughter of the famous
champion. Nuline is an
Anglicized form of Nuallain,
meaning famous champion or
charioteer. See Nola.

Oanez
(Wah-nez)
Pure. Oanez is a Breton variant
of Agnes, derived from the word
'oan' and the Latin 'agnus',
meaning lamb.

Oifa
(Ee-fah)
Meaning unknown. In Irish mythology, Oifa replaced her dead sister Ove as the wife of Lir and turned her stepchildren into swans.

Oona
(Oo-na)
Pure and chaste, or hunger, or lamb, or one. Oona has several possible origins. The Gaelic 'una' means hunger, while 'uan' means lamb. It could be derived from the Latin 'una', meaning one, or, as a variant of Oonagh, from Agnes, which means pure and chaste.

Oonagh
(Oo-na)
Pure and chaste. See Oona. In Irish mythology, Oonagh was Queen of the Fairies and the wife of Fionn Mac Cool.

Ove
(Oh-veh)
Meaning unknown, though it can be a derivation of the Greek Ovalia (Ophelia), meaning help. Ove was the mythical daughter of Dearg and sister of Oifa, who died in labour.

Padraigin
(Pah-dreeg-in)
Of noble birth. A variant of Patricia, from Latin origins meaning upper class, Padraigin is the female form of boys' name Pádraig.

Padriga
(Pah-dree-gah)
Of noble birth. A variant of Padraigin.

Paola
(Pow-la)
Small and humble. A Breton form of the name Paula, originally derived from the Roman name Paulus.

Piala
(Pee-a-la)
Caution. Piala is a Breton and Cornish name, possibly derived from the Welsh for prudence.

Raghnailt
(Rayn-ilt)

All knowing. Raghnailt is derived from the Old Norse words 'regin', meaning advice, and 'hildr' meaning battle.

Regan
(Ray-gun or Ree-gun)
Furious or impulsive, or queen. Regan is derived from the Irish Riagan. It also has associations with the word 'regina', meaning queen. Regan can also be a boys' name.

Reghan
(Ray-gun or Ree-gun)
Furious or impulsive, or queen. See Regan.

Rhedyn
(Red-in)
A Welsh name meaning fern.

Rhegan
(Ray-gun or Ree-gun)
Furious or impulsive, or queen. See Regan.

Riona
(Ree-in-ock or Ree-oh-na)
Regal girl. Riona is derived from the Gaelic 'rionach', meaning queenly. In mythology,

Rioghnach was the wife of Irish king Niall of the Nine Hostages and was known as an ancestor to many prominent names, such as the MacLoughlins and O'Donnells.

Rionach
(Ree-uh-nak)
Regal girl. See Riona.

Ronana
(Roh-nah-nah)
Little seal. Ronana is the female version of the boys' name Ronan.

Ronat
(Roh-nat)
Little seal. A variant of Ronana.

Sadh
(Sayve)
Sweet and good.

Sadhbh
(Sayve)
Sweet and good. A variant of Sadh.

Saoirse
(Seer-sha)
Freedom and liberty. A very popular name in Ireland.

Sadhbh: the deer

The lover of Fionn Mac Cool, Sadhbh was turned into a deer after refusing the charms of dark druid Fer Doirich. After three years, one of his servants helped her escape Fer's clutches by sending her to the Fianna's castle, where the dark druid had no power over her. Beautiful once more, she married Fionn, who gave up all pleasures for her. She gave birth to Oisin, but again fell prey to Fer, who turned her into a deer once more and she was lost forever.

Saraid
(Sor-id)
An Irish name meaning the best, or surpassing all.

Seasaidh
(Sess-ee)
God is gracious. Seasaidh is a variant of the Scottish Jessie.

Seirian
(Se-reen)
A name of Irish and Welsh origins meaning sparkling.

Selma
(Sel-ma)
Helmet of God. Selma is an abbreviation of the Germanic name Anselma.

Seonag
(Sho-nah)
God is gracious. Seonag is a Gaelic variant of Shona and Janet, from the Hebrew Joan.

Seonaid
(Sho-nah)
God is gracious. See Seonag.

Sererena
(Seh-reh-ree-na)
A Cornish name meaning calm, probably derived from the Latin Serena, meaning serene.

Shauna
(Shaw-na)
God's gracious gift. Shauna is a feminine variant of Sean, which itself is derived from the biblical name John.

Sheena
(Shee-nah)
God is gracious. See Sheenagh.

Sheenagh
(Shee-nah)
God is gracious. Sheenagh is an Irish form of Jane.

Shibley
(Shib-lee)
God is my oath.

Shona
(Sho-nah)
God is gracious. A Scottish version of Joan. See Seonag.

Sian
(Shahn)
God is gracious. Sian is a Welsh version of Jane.

Sine
(Seen)
God is gracious. See Sheenagh and Sian.

Sinead
(Shin-aid)
God is gracious. A variant of Jane, and a diminutive form of Siobhan.

Siobhan
(Sha-vawn)
God is gracious. Siobhan is an Irish name derived from the Old French Jehanne, which itself was a variant of Joan.

Siomha
(Shee-vah)
A time of peace. Siomha is a variant of the Irish name Síthmaith, derived from the word 'síth' for peace and 'maith' for good.

Sorcha
(Sor-ha or Sor-ka)
Bright light.

Sulgwenn
(Sool-gwen)
Shining sun. Sulgwenn is an
Old Breton name, derived from
the word 'sul' meaning sun and
'gwen' for white.

Taillte
(Tal-the)
Meaning unknown. Taillte
was the Irish earth goddess of
August, who was married to a
High King of Ireland, foster
mother to Lugh, god of light,
and is said to have lived on the
Hill of Tara. The Irish town of
Telltown is named after her and
the Tailteann Games were held
annually in her honour.

Tangwystl
(Tang-wist-el)
A Welsh name meaning pledge of
peace.

Tierney
(Teer-nee)
Noble. Tierney is derived from
the Gaelic word for lord.
Tierney is also a boys' name.

Trifin
(Tree-feen)
Meaning unknown. Trifin is a

UNA AND THE DRAGON

In Edmund Spenser's homage to Elizabeth I, *The Faery
Queen*, Una represents truth and joins forces with a
Red Cross Knight and a dwarf to rescue her parents
from a dragon. Their adventure finds them overcoming
wickedness and lies, until eventually they remember the
value of honour and mercy and are rewarded with joy.

Breton name associated with mythology, including the tale of Bluebeard. St Trifin is the patron saint of sick children.

Trifine
(Tree-fee-nah)
See Trifin.

Tristana
(Tris-tah-na)
Tumult, din, or sad. Tristana is a female version of the boys' name Tristan.

Una
(Oo-nah)
Pure and chaste, or hunger, or lamb, or one. Oona has several possible origins. The Gaelic 'una' means hunger, while 'uan' means lamb. On the other hand, it could be derived from the Latin 'una', meaning one, or, as a variant of Oonagh, from Agnes, which means pure and chaste.
See Oona.

Valma
(Val-ma)
Helmet, protection. Valma is derived from the Old Norse Valda, Velda and Velma, and also the Germanic Wilma.

Yanna
(Yan-na)
God is gracious. Yanna is a Cornish and Breton name derived from the Hebrew Yoana.

PHYSICAL FEATURES

This chapter consists of names that describe a girl's appearance or stature. In some cases this is implied by an object meaning, such as rampart.

Aelwen
(Isle-wen)
A Welsh name meaning fair of brow or blessed brow.

Ailbhe
(Al-beh or Al-veh)
White. See Ailbe.

Ailsa
(ale-sah)
Ailsa Craig is a craggy island in the Firth of Clyde and it is from this that the name is thought to be taken, though it is also a variant of the Hebrew name Elsa, meaning God's promise. Ailsa Craig means the island of Alfsigr, Alfsigr being Old Norse for elfin victory or magical victory.

Aislin
(Ash-ling)
A popular name in Ireland today, Aislin means a vision or dream.

Aislinn
(Ash-ling)
A vision or dream. See Aislin.

Aleen
(A-leen)
A Celtic form of Helen and a feminine version of Allen, Aleen means light, as in sunny or fair, and is associated with good looks. In Scottish usage Aleen could be derived from Aileen and is used to mean lovely.

Aleena
(A-leen-ah)
Light and attractive. See Aleen.

Alena
(A-lay-na)
Light and attractive. See Aleen.

Alina
(A-leen-ah)
Light and attractive. See Aleen.

Aline
(A-leen-ah)
Light and attractive. See Aleen.

Allena
(A-leen-ah)
Light and attractive. See Aleen.

Allene
(A-leen-ah)
Light and attractive. See Aleen.

Almeda
(Al-mee-da)
In Wales the name Almeda means shapely, while in Brittany it is less of a physical description and more of a character one: good, kind or lovable.

Anabla
(An-ab-la)
A Celtic equivalent of the French Annabelle, Anabla means beautiful Ana.

Anwen
(An-wen)
A Welsh name meaning very fair or very beautiful.

Aobh
(Eve)
Radiant beauty.

Aobhinn
(Ee-vin)
Radiant beauty. Aobhinn is a pet form of Aobh, as in little Aobh. In the Middle Ages, Aobhinn was a common name among princesses, and has enjoyed renewed popularity in the 21st century.

Aoibheann
(Ee-vin)
Radiant beauty. See Aobhinn.

Aoibhell
(Ee-fel)
Beautiful. A derivation of Aoibhinn. In Irish mythology, Aoibhell was a fairy queen of North Munster, who possessed a magical harp that brought about the death of anybody who heard it.

Aoife
(Ee-fa)
A very popular name in Ireland, meaning beautiful and radiant.

In the Irish legend *The Children of Lir*, Aoife was the name of the king's second wife, who became jealous of her step-children's love for their father and for one another and turned them into swans. When her father Bodb found out what she had done, he turned her into a crow. But Aoife is also the name of a great warrior from Irish mythology. She was reputed to be the greatest woman warrior in the world, but was defeated in combat by the Ulster hero Cu Chulainn and went on to bear him a son, Connlach.

Aouregan
(Ow-ray-gahn)

White, pure or fair, either in appearance or nature. Aouregan comes from the Breton 'aour' meaning gold and 'gwenn' meaning shining or holy.

Aouregwenn
(Ow-ray-gwen)

White, pure or fair. See Aouregan.

Argantlon
(Ahr-gahnt-lon)

A Breton name derived from the words 'argant', meaning silver or shining, and 'lon' meaning full.

Argantlowen
(Ahr-gahnt-lo-wen)

A Breton name derived from the words 'argant', meaning silver or shining, and 'lowen' meaning joyful.

Ariana
(Ari-ah-na)

A name of Welsh origin meaning silver.

Arianrhod
(Ari-an-trod)

A Welsh name meaning silver wheel, which can be taken to mean moon. Arianrhod was the goddess of the moon in Welsh mythology.

Arzhela
(Ar-zay-la)

Bear princess. A feminine form of Arzhel, with similar origins to Armelle.

Ashling
(Ash-ling)
A vision or dream. See Aislin.

Aziliz
(Ah-zee-leez)
A Breton name derived from the Welsh name Seissylt, meaning sixth, and a variant of Cecilia.

Bedelia
(Be-de-li-ya)
Strong, heavenly or exalted one. Bedelia is a variant of the name Brighid, which is Anglicized to Bridget. In Irish mythology, Brighid was a goddess. Saint Brigid of Kildare is one of Ireland's patron saints.

Beibhinn
(Be-veen)
A name that occurs more than once in Irish mythology, Beibhinn means fair lady, referring specifically to hair colour. It was a name used to describe Viking women. Beibhinn was the mother of Brian Boru, who also gave his daughter the same name. In another legend, Beibhinn was a golden-haired giantess who sought protection with Fionn Mac Cool.

Berit
(Bay-rit)
Splendid, magnificent or lovely.

Berneen
(Bur-neen)
A derivation of the name Bernadine, which in turn is a feminine form of the boys' name Bernard, which means strong or brave bear.

Berta
(Bair-ta)
Splendid, magnificent or lovely. A variant of Berit.

Bevin
(Bay-vin)
Fair lady. An Anglicized form of the name Beibhinn.

Birgit
(Bur-git)
Splendid or strong. A variant of Brighid.

BLAITHNAID AND THE COW

In Celtic legend, Blaithnaid is married to the magical king Cu Raoi Mac Daire, who takes her from her true love Cu Chulainn against her will. Blaithnaid and Cu Chulainn plot to kill Cu Raoi and hatch a plan for Blaithnaid to give a signal when the fortress is poorly defended. She does so by milking her cow and letting the milk run down from the fortress into the stream, showing the way for Cu Chulainn to launch his raid and rescue his beloved. With Cu Raoi dead, they return to Ulster. But Feircheirtne, a druid loyal to Cu Raoi, grabs Blaithnaid and jumps off a cliff with her in his arms, killing them both.

Birkita
(Bur-kit-a)
Strong. A variant of Brighid.

Birte
(Bur-ta)
Splendid, magnificent or lovely. A variant of Berit.

Blaine
(Blayn)
From the word 'bla' meaning yellow, Blaine is a Scottish name meaning little yellow one, a reference to hair colour. It can also mean slender and may be a variant of Blane, the name of a 7th-century Scottish saint.

Blaithin
(Blah-heen)
Flower or blossom. A name derived from the word 'blath',

meaning both flower and
blossom. Blaithin is a variant of
Blaithnaid.

Blanaid

(Blaw-nid)
Flower or blossom. See Blaithin.

Blathnaid

(Blaw-nid)
Flower or blossom. See Blaithin.
Blaithnaid was a character in
Irish mythology, who fell in love
with Cu Chulainn.

Bleuzenn

(Bloo-zen)
From the Breton word for flower.
The Breton feast of St Bleuzenn
is on 24 November.

Blodeuwedd

(Blod-doo-widh)
Flower or blossom face.
Originally spelt Blodeuedd, she was
a flower bride from medieval Welsh
Mabinogion legend who had an
affair and was turned into an owl.
The name changed to Blodeuwedd,
meaning flower face, because of the
markings around her owl eyes.

Blodwen

(Blo-dwen)
Welsh Celtic name meaning
white flower, derived from
the Gaelic word 'blodyn' for
flower and 'gwyn' for white and
blessed. A variant of Blodwyn and
Blodwynne.

Boann

(Bo-ann)
Celtic name of uncertain origin,
thought to come from the
Irish for white cow. A variant of
Bo-Ann, Boanne and Bo-Anne.

Brangaine

(Brang-eena)
Fair beauty.
Brangaine was the servant of
the princess Isolde in the tale
of Tristan and Isolde. A variant
of Brangaene, Brangwane and
Brangien.

Branna

(Bran-ah)
Raven. Gaelic for dark-haired
beauty.

BOANN: IRISH GODDESS OF FERTILITY AND THE RIVER BOYNE

The wife of Nechtan the water god, Boann has a secret affair with powerful protector the Dagda, which is hidden from her husband by making the sun stay still for nine months so their son can be conceived, gestated and born in a day. Tempting fate again, another tale is that Boann challenges the magical Well of Wisdom, forbidden to her by her husband, causing its waters to rage violently and take her life. Hence she remains as goddess of the resultant lake.

Brannagh
(Bran-ah)
Raven beauty. See Branna.

Branwen
(Bran-wen)
Dark blessed beauty.
Sister of Bendigeidfran and
daughter of Llyr in medieval
Welsh Mabinogion legend,
Branwen was married to the
cruel Matholwch, king of Ireland.
A variant of Brangwen and
Bronwen.

Breage
(Bray-ga)
Fine and lovely.

Brenda
(Bren-dah)
Of Norse origin, meaning sword.
Thought to be the female version of
Brendan or from the Viking term
'brand', meaning bright sword.

Brenna
(Bren-ah)
Raven. See Branna.

Briallen
(Bree-ah-len)
Welsh name meaning primrose.

Camryn
(Cam-rin)
Meaning crooked nose, and a variant of the Scottish boys' clan name Cameron.

Caoilainn
(Kay-lin or Koy-lin)
Fair and slender. Caoilainn is a variant of Caoilfhinn, a popular Irish saint's name, also giving it a meaning of purity.

Caoilfhinn
(Kay-lin or Kee-lin)
Fair and slender. See Caoilainn.

Caoimhe
(Kwee-va or Kee-va)
From the word 'caomh', meaning beautiful and gentle, this is a popular Irish and Scottish name, derived from the boys' name Kevin.

Cassidy
(Kass-id-ee)
Curly, or clever. A derivation of Caiside, from the Gaelic for curly hair, and also said to be someone who is clever.

Ciara
(Kee-rah)
Dark, usually relating to eyes, hair or skin. A variant of Keera, Keira and Kira. Ciara is the female version of boys' name Ciarán and also the saint name of the 7th-century Irish nun who founded a monastery in Kilkeary.

Cigfa
(Kig-fa)
Raven, which generally relates to the eyes, hair or skin colouring.

Cinnia
(Sin-ee-a)
Beauty. Variant of Cinnie, which comes from the Greek Cynthia, derived from Mount Kynthos.

Cinnie
(Sin-ee)
Beauty. See Cinnia.

THE GODDESS WHO FELL IN LOVE WITH A MORTAL

There are a number of variations on the tales of Cliodhna. A beautiful love goddess from Irish legend, she was a daughter of poet Libra, who gave up the Land of Promise when she fell for mortal man Ciabhan, also known as Keevan of the Curling Locks. But once ashore to be with him, she was swept away by a fatal wave sent by the god of the sea.

Claire

(Klare)
From the Latin name meaning clear and bright, and introduced to Britain by the Normans. St Clare, disciple of Francis of Assisi, founded the 'Poor Clares' order of Catholic nuns, which became well respected in Ireland. See also variants Ceara and Ciara.

Clarisant

(Klar-ees-ant)
Clear and bright. See Claire.

Cliodhna

(Klee-on-a)
Beautiful. Cliodhna is derived from the word 'clodhna', meaning slender.

Cliona

(Klee-o-na)
Beautiful. See of Cliodhna.

Daire

(Dah-rah)
Oak tree, or fruitful. Daire is a favoured name of Irish legends, female and male. A variant of Dara.

Daireann
(Dar-rawn)
Bountiful and fruitful. The
beautiful young Daireann fell
in love with Fionn Mac Cool,
the biggest giant in Scotland.
He already had many wives but
she asked to be his only wife for
a year, settling for half of his
time after. A variant of Dairine,
Darran and Darina.

Dara
(Dah-ra)
Oak tree. See Daire.

Darcy
(Dah-see)
Dark one, implying a physical
trait, such as dark eyes, hair or
skin. Darcy is derived from the
Irish word 'dorcha' for dark,
or a descendant of the dark
one. Also a surname, variants
include Darcie and English
Dorcey.

Darfhinn
(Dar-rin)
Golden-haired daughter or
daughter of Finn.

Delia
(Deel-ya)
Dark. A name of Welsh origin,
and also derived from Bedelia,
a variant of Bridget, the Celtic
goddess of fire and poetry, and
the English Odelia. See Cordelia.

Donia
(Don-ya)
Dark-skinned, or ruler of the world.

Duana
(Dwah-na)
Dark and swarthy. Duana is the
female version of the boys' name
Duane. Also associated with the
meaning melody.

Dubh Lacha
(Doov-lock-a)
A dark beautiful maiden of the
lake, or a black duck.
Dubh Lacha is a mythological
Irish sea fairy or mermaid.
These ocean maidens were
known for luring men into their
waters with their irresistible
charms.

Duibheasa
(Doo-veh-sah)

DUBH LACHA OF THE WHITE ARMS

Renowned for her fair limbs, Dubh Lacha was married to Mongán, who had been born on the same day as her. Desired by Brandub, he tricked her husband into parting with her. But turning herself into a beauty Brandub couldn't resist, Cuimne the hag played the same game to help Mongán retrieve his wife, after which she reverted to her usual form.

Dark lady of the waterfall. A medieval name that can also be spelt Dubheasa.

Duibhghiolla
(Doo-vil-ah)
Dark lady of Lemain. Duibhghiolla was the wife of High King Donnchad Mac Flaind.

Eibhleann
(Ave-lin)
Radiant and beautiful. Eibhleann is derived from the Norman Aveline.

Eibhlin
(Eve-lin or Ev-lin)
Radiant and beautiful. A variant of Eibhleann. A popular piece of music at Irish weddings, 'Eibhlin a Ruan' was composed by 17th-century harpist Cearbhall O'Dalaigh to woo his love away from her wedding day to elope with him.

Eileen
(Aye-leen)
Radiant and beautiful. A form of Helen. See also Eibhleann.

Eilwen
(Al-win)
Fair brow. Eilwen is derived from
the Welsh word 'ael', meaning
brow, and 'gwen', meaning white
or blessed.

Eimear
(Ee-mer)
Swift. Eimear is derived from
the Gaelic word 'eimh' and is a
simplified form of Eimhear.

Einin
(Aye-neen)
Little bird.

Eirwen
(Air-wen)
A Welsh name meaning snow
white.

Eluned
(El-oon-ed)
Idol or image. Eluned is a Welsh
name for an object of desire. A
variant of Luned. Saint Eluned
was a 5th-century Welsh saint.

Emer
(Aim-er)
Swift. See Eimear.

Ena
(Eh-nah)
Nut, kernel or fire. Ena is a
variant of Eithne and Aednat.

Esyllt
(Ess-ilt)
Exceptionally beautiful. Thought
to be of Welsh origin meaning fair
lady, though also associated with
Old French and Germanic roots.
Also a variant of Iseult, Isolde and
Yseult.

Ethne
(Et-na)
Nut or fire. See Eithne.

Eurwen
(Air-wen)
A Welsh name meaning golden
girl, from the words 'aur' or
'euraid', meaning gold, and
'gwyn' for white and blessed.

Evelyn
(Ee-veh-lin or Eh-veh-lin)

EMER OF THE SIX GIFTS

In Irish mythology, Emer is blessed with the Six Gifts of Womanhood: beauty, voice, words, wisdom, needlework and chastity. As children, she and the warrior Cu Chulainn love each other dearly, but although later as his wife she accepts the nature of his wandering eye, she cannot cope when he makes love to Fand, wife of sea god Manannan. When she sees how deep their love is, she nobly offers to leave, but her unselfishness touches Fand, who goes back to the sea alone.

Light or bird. Also used as a boys' name, though rare. See Evelina.

Fenella
(Feh-neh-la)
Fair-shouldered and beautiful. A variant of Fionnuala, derived from 'fionn', meaning white, and 'guala' for shoulder.

Ffion
(Fee-on)
Fair and beautiful. Ffion is the Welsh Gaelic equivalent of Fiona.

Fflur
(Flur)
A Welsh name meaning flowers.

Findabair
(Finn-dab-air)
Fair eyebrows, fair portion, or a white phantom. In Irish legend, Findabair is a heroine who only loves once, and the mythical daughter of Medb of Connacht.

Finnguala

(Fin-gwah-la)
Fair-shouldered and beautiful,
a very popular Irish name in
the early Middle Ages and
the full version of Nuala. See
Fenella.

Finola

(Fin-oh-la)
Fair-shouldered and beautiful.
Anglicized version of Fionnuala.
See Fenella.

Fiona

(Fee-oh-na)
Fair and beautiful. See Ffion.

Fionnuala

(Fee-on-nwa-la)
Fair-shouldered and beautiful.
See Fenella.

Fionnula

(Fee-on-oo-la)
Irish and Gaelic name, meaning
fair-shouldered and beautiful. See
Fenella.

FIONNUALA SAVED BY THE BELL

King Lir and his wife Aobh had a daughter Fionnoula and three sons Aedh, Conn and Fiachra. However, following the death of Aobh, Lir's second wife, the jealous Aoife, turned the children into swans for 300 years on Lake Daravarragh, 300 years on the Sea of Moyle and 300 years on Innis Glora. Only the sound of a Christian bell in Ireland would save them. When St Patrick arrived, the children were saved by the bell and baptized by him.

Flanna
(Flan-na)
Red or russet, usually relating to hair colour.

Gaynor
(Gay-nor)
Fair and beautiful. Gaynor is the Anglicized version of Guinevere, derived from the words 'gwen' for white and 'hwyfar' for smooth, and of Norman French origin.

Genevieve
(Jen-eh-veev or Jen-eh-vyev)
English version of the French name Geneviève, meaning white wave or tribeswoman.

Germaine
(Jer-main)
Loud voice. Germaine is almost certainly of French origin, derived from the Latin for brother. Germaine was a 16th-century saint. It can also be used as a boys' name.

Gethan
(Geth-an)
Dark, dusky. Gethan is a female form of the Welsh boys' name Gethan.

Ginebra
(Gin-eh-bra)
White, fair lady, or juniper tree. Ginebra is a variant of Guinevere, but could also be derived from the Old French for juniper tree.

Ginerva
(Gin-er-va)
White, fair lady. A variant of Guinevere.

Ginessa
(Gin-ess-er)
White, fair lady. A variant of Guinevere.

Giorsal
(Gur-sul)
Grey-haired. Giorsal is a Scottish variant of Griselda, which means grey-haired. Also a variant of Grizel.

Gitta
(Gi-tah)
Strong, Gitta is an abbreviated form of the Germanic Brigitta, a variant of Bridget.

Gobhnet
(Gub-nidge)
Of uncertain meaning, thought
to be a Gaelic name derived
from the Irish word 'gob' for
mouth, and the Irish equivalent
of Barbara, meaning foreign
woman.

Guenevere
(Gwen-a-vere)
White lady, fair and pure.
A variant of Guinevere and
the popular Cornish version,
Jennifer.

Guennola
(Gwen-oh-la)
White lady, fair and smooth. A
variant of Guinevere and Gwen.

Guinevere
(Gwin-a-vere)
White lady, fair and smooth.
See Guenevere. Lady Guinevere
was the legendary wife of King
Arthur.

Gwen
(Gwen)
White, fair and pure. A Welsh
name from the word 'gwyn',
meaning white and blessed, often
an abbreviated form of longer
names such as Gwendolen and
Guenevere etc.

Gwencalon
(Gwayn-ka-lon)
An Old Breton name, derived
from the words 'gwenn' for
bright and shining, and 'calon'
for heart.

Gwendolen
(Gwen-doh-len)
White circle or moon. Of
Welsh origin, meaning white
circle or moon, from the words
'gwen' for fair and blessed, and
'dolen' for ring or bow. See
Gwen. Gwendolen is the name
of Merlin's wife in Arthurian
legend and also a medieval moon
goddess.

Gwendolyn
(Gwen-doh-lin)
White circle or moon. See
Gwendolen.

Gweneira
(Gwen-eh-ra)
Snow white and pure. See Gwen.

GUINEVERE, ARTHUR'S QUEEN

According to legend, King Arthur's fair queen was not so fair in love and war. When she fell for Sir Lancelot, their affair resulted in the Battle of Camlann – and her husband's death. Arthur was warned by the sons of King Lot and ordered she be burned at the stake, knowing the flown Lancelot would return and attempt to save her. Which he did. However, the plan went awry when Gawain's brothers were killed during the rescue. He encouraged a war between Arthur and Lancelot, with fatal consequences to the kingdom. Guinevere was left in the 'care' of crown-seeking Mordred and accepted his evil offer of marriage, but escaped to a convent where she remained for the rest of her life. Arthur had the traitor Mordred killed, but could not survive his own wounds.

Gweneth
(Gwen-eth)
Fair and pure. See Gwen.

Gwenith
(Gwen-ith)
Fair and pure. See Gwen.

Gwenllian
(Gwen-lee-an)
Popular royal Welsh name, meaning blonde and flaxen, from the word 'llian'. See Gwen.

Gwenneth
(Gwen-neth)
Fair and pure. See Gwen.

Gwenonwyn
(Gwen-on-win)
Lily of the valley.

Gwenyver
(Gwen-iv-ear)
White lady, fair and pure. See
Guenevere and Gwen.

Gwyndolin
(Gwin-doh-lin)
White circle or moon. See Gwen.

Gwynne
(Gwin)
White lady, fair and pure. See
Guenevere and Gwen.
Also used as a boys' name.

Hafwen
(Haf-win)
A Welsh name meaning summer
beauty.

Ia
(Ee-a)
Violet flowers.
Ia was a 13th-century Irish
princess who became a Cornish
saint.

Igerna
(Eye-gur-na)
Fair lady. Igerna is a variant of
the Welsh name Ygerna, and
possibly of the Old English
Igrayne, the name of King
Arthur's mother.

Ineda
(Ee-nay-da)
Nut or fire.

Ione
(Eye-oh-nee or Eye-ohne)
Island. A variant of Iona.

Iseult
(Ay-sult or Iss-ult)
Beautiful and fair. Iseult (or
Isolde) was an Irish princess of
Arthurian legend – see the Old
Irish variant Essylt.

Isolda
Beautiful and fair. Latinized
version of Isolde. See Iseult.

Isolde
(Ee-zold)
Beautiful and fair. See Iseult.

TRISTAN AND ISEULT

Irish princess Iseult (also Isolde, Yseult, among other variations) was promised to King Mark of Cornwall but fell in love with his Cornish knight Tristan. Their affair led to their deaths via a Romeo and Juliet-style poisonous vial. The story is thought to have influenced the legend of Guinevere and Lancelot, and is also told in Wagner's opera and more recently a Hollywood movie.

Isolt
(Ee-solt)
Beautiful and fair. See Iseult.

Ivori
(Eye-vor-ee)
Of English origin, a variant of Ivory. Also the Welsh female version of boys' name Ivor.

Jenny
(Jen-ee)
Fair and pure or white wave. See Jennifer.

Jennyfer
(Jen-i-fer)
Fair and pure or white wave. See Jennifer.

Jennyver
(Jen-i-ver)
Fair and pure or white wave. See Jennifer.

Keela
(Kee-la)
Beautiful and graceful. Keela is a variant of the Irish name Cadhla.

Keelia

(Kee-lee-a)
Slender and pretty. A variant of
Keely.

Keelin

(Kee-lin)
Slender and pretty. See Keelia.

Keely

(Kee-lee)
Slender and pretty. See Keelia.

Keera

(Kee-ra)
Dark. See Ciara.

Keira

(Kee-ra)
Dark. See Ciara.

Kennocha

(Ken-oh-ca)
An Irish name meaning lovely.

Keri

(Keh-ree)
Dark. A variant of Kerry. See
Ciara.

Kerry

(Keh-ree)
Dark. See Ciara.
County Kerry, the Anglicized
version of the Gaelic Chiarrai,
means 'land of the people of
Ciar', who was the son of High
King Fergus Mac Róich.

Keyne

(Keen)
A variant of the Welsh name
Ceinwen, meaning beautiful
and blessed. Also thought to
be a Cornish name meaning
knowledgeable.

Kiera

(Kee-ra)
Dark. See Ciara.

Kira

(Kee-ra)
Dark. See Ciara.

Kyla

(Keye-la)
Slender, or beautiful. Kyla means
narrow or slender, as in a strait
of water (the Kyle of Lochalsh),
or can be a variant of the Irish
Cadhla, meaning beautiful,

graceful. See Keela. Kyla is a female version of boys' name Kyle.

Kyra
(Key-ra)
Dark. A variant of Ciara.

Laban
(La-ban)
White. Laban is a name of Hebrew origin.

Lachtna
(Luck-na)
An Irish Gaelic name, meaning milk-coloured and pure. Lachtna is usually a boys' name.

Lana
(La-na or Law-na)
Little rock. A variant of the Germanic name Alana, meaning precious, and the Latinized female version of the boys' name Alan.

Lasair
(Las-air)
Flame or blaze, usually relating to red hair.

Liobhan
(Lee-von)
Female beauty.
Liobhan was the wife of Lúathlám in the Ulster Tales.

Llian
(Hlee-an)
Of uncertain origin, thought to refer to golden hair.

Luighseach
(Loo-see)
Radiant or torch bringer. A variant of Lucy, this is also the female version of boys' name Lug, probably after the heroic mythological Irish god Lugh.

Luiseach
(Loo-see)
Radiant or torch bringer. See Luighseach.

Mabina
(Mab-ee-na)
An Irish name meaning nimble.

Maeveen
(May-veen)
Nimble.

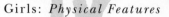

Mairead
(Ma-raid or Muh-raid)
Pearl. Mairead is the Irish and
Scottish equivalent of Margaret.

Maiwen
(My-win)
A Welsh name meaning beautiful
Mary.

Malvina
(Mal-vee-na)
A Scottish name meaning smooth
brow, or sweet in Irish.

Marc'harit
(Mahr-xahr-eed)
Pearl. A popular Breton form of
Margaret.

Marsali
(Mar-sal-ee)
Pearl. Marsali is a Scottish variant
of Margaret and Marjorie.

Maureen
(Mor-een)
White, fair, or sea. Maureen is
a variant of the Irish Muireann,
but also a pet form of the biblical
name Mary.

Meadghbh
(Mayv)
Nimble. A variant of Maebh.

Melva
(Mel-va)
Slender, delicate, smooth
browed.

Melvina
(Mel-vee-na)
Slender, delicate, smooth
browed. See Melva.

Miniver
(Min-iv-er)
Beautiful, or white, fair.
Miniver is possibly derived from
Minerva, the Roman goddess of
wisdom, or could be a variant
of Guinevere, from the Welsh
words 'gwyn' meaning white and
'hwyfar' meaning smooth.

Morvana
(Mor-var-nah)
Pale. Morvana is a female version
of boys' name Morvan.

Niamh
(Neev or Nee-ev)
Bright and radiant.

NIAMH OF THE GOLDEN HAIR

Niamh Chinn Oir appears in the Finn Tales as a beautiful sea goddess, daughter of sea god Manannan, and is known for her beauty, fair locks and riding a white horse. When she falls in love with Fionn Mac Cool's son Oisin, she tempts him to the Land of Promise and Eternal Youth for what he thinks is three weeks, but is in fact 300 years.

Niamh is a popular Irish name, after a goddess from Irish mythology. Anglicized versions include Niav and Neave.

Nola
(Noh-la)
Fair-shouldered and beautiful, or daughter of the famous champion. Nola is an abbreviation of the name Finola, meaning white shoulder, and can also mean a descendant of Nuallain, a name that means famous champion or charioteer. The latter is the equivalent of the boys' name Nolan.

Nuala
(Noo-la)
Fair-shouldered and beautiful. Nuala is an abbreviated form of Fionnuala.

Oighrig
(Ef-rik)
New spotted or speckled one. A variant of the Gaelic Aithbhreac.

Olwen
(Ol-wen)
A Welsh name meaning white footprint. Olwen is derived from the words 'ol' and 'gwen', meaning white.

In Welsh mythology, Olwen was the daughter of Welsh giant Yspaddaden and wherever she went, white clover would grow beneath her feet.

Olwyn
(Ol-win)
White footprint. See Olwen.

Orchil
(Or-hill)
Dark-haired one, or prayer.

Oriana
(Or-ee-ah-na)
Golden, or sunrise. Oriana is a Celtic name of Latin origins, from 'or', meaning gold, usually referring to hair colour.

Orla
(Or-lah)
Golden princess. Orla is an Anglicized variant of Orfhlaith, from the Irish words 'or' for gold and 'flaith' for princess. A popular Irish name, Orla was a grand niece of Irish High King Brian Boru.

Orlagh
(Or-lah)
Golden princess. See Orla.

Orlaith
(Or-lah)
Golden princess. See Orla.

Ornait
(Or-nit)
Sallow or green. Ornait is an Irish variant of Ornat, meaning little pale-green one. It is the Anglicized version of Odharnait. In Irish history, Ornait was a queen of Connacht and a princess of Munster.

Penarddun
(Pen-ard-dun)
Most beautiful. Penarddun is derived from the Welsh words 'pen' for foremost and 'arddun' for fair. In the Welsh Mabinogion legend, Penarddun is the daughter of Beli Mawr.

Radha
(Rad-ha or Roh-a)
Vision. Radha is derived from the

Irish word 'radharc', meaning view or vision.

Rhianwen

(Ree-an-wen)

Fair or comely maiden. A Welsh name from 'rhian', meaning maiden, and 'gwen', meaning fair.

Rhonwen

(Ron-win)

White lance or fair hair.

Roisin

(Rosh-een)

Little rose. Roisin is an Irish name from Latin origins.

Rosaleen

(Roz-a-leen)

Little red-head, or little rose.

Rowen

(Roe-en)

White and slender, or little red-head. Rowen can be a derivation of the Welsh words 'rhon', meaning spike, and 'gwen', meaning white, or from a Gaelic origin meaning red. Rowen is also a boys' name.

Rowena

(Roe-een-a)

White and slender, or little red-head. See Rowen.

Rozenn

(Roh-zen)

A Breton name meaning rose.

Ruari

(Roo-ir-ree)

Red queen or poet. Ruari is the female version of Rory.

Scathach

(Scah-hah)

Faint, or sheltered and shady. Scathach was a Scottish female warrior in Irish mythology, said to have taught combat arts to Irish hero Cu Chulainn. The island of Skye is said to be named after her.

Seirial

(Se-reel)

Sparkling. A variant of Seirian.

Senga

(Sen-gah)

Pure and slender. Senga is a Scottish name using the reverse of Greek name Agnes, meaning pure and chaste.

Sheila
(Shee-la)
Sixth child. An Anglicized form of Sheelagh.

Sile
(Shee-lah)
Sixth child. A variant of Sheelagh.

Steren
(Stay-ren)
A Cornish name meaning star.

Sterenn
(Stay-ren)
Star. A Breton variant of the Cornish Steren.

Teagan

(Tee-gan)
Pretty and poetic. A Gaelic name used in England and Ireland, meaning little poet and philosopher, and with Welsh origins in the variant Tegan, meaning beautiful. Also used as a boys' name.

Teagin
(Tee-gin)
Pretty and poetic. See Teagan.

Tegan
(Tee-gan or Teg-an)
Beautiful and good. See Teagan.

Tegwen
(Teg-wen)
Beautiful and good. See Teagan and Tegan.

Ula
(Oo-la)
Jewel of the sea, or wealthy

Valmai
(Val-may)
A Welsh name meaning mayflower.

Vevila
(Ve-vee-la)
Harmony, or melodic of voice.

Winnie
(Win-ee)
Blessed and fair. Winnie is short for Winifred and Gwyneth.

Wynne

(Win)

Blessed and fair. See Gwyneth.
Wynne is also a boys' name.

Wynnie

(Win-nee)

Blessed and fair. See Winnie.

Yseult

(Ee-solt)

Beautiful and fair. A variant of
Iseult.

Zenevieva

(Zen-eh-vyeh-va)

White wave or tribeswoman. A
variant of Genevieve.

Zinerva

(Zin-er-vah)

White wave or tribeswoman. See
Zenevieva.

PLACES

This chapter features girls' names that are inspired by a place, landmark or natural feature. Many of these names would have originated as surnames, which were often derived from the place a person lived or came from.

Avenie
(A-vay-nee)
Derived from the Celtic word 'avon', meaning river.

Blair
(Blayr)
A Scottish name meaning plain or field, it would have referred to people who came from the plain or from the field.
Blair is also a boys' name and a surname.

Bret
(Bret)
A girl from Britain or Brittany. A variant of the Latin Brett and Brittany.

Bretta
(Bret-ta)
From Britain or Brittany. See Bret.

Brit
(Brit)
Exalted, or from Britain or Brittany. Also thought to mean spotted and freckled, a variant of Brittany. See Bret.

Brita
(Bree-ta)
Exalted one. See Bret and Bridget.

Brittany
(Brit-an-ee)
From Britain or Brittany. See Bret.

Brynna
(Brin-ah)
Little hill. Brynna is derived from the Welsh 'bryn'.

Clodagh
(Klo–da)
Popular Irish name derived from the river Clody, which runs through County Tipperary and County Wexford. Possibly a variant of the Latin Claudia.

Dailigh
(Day-lee)
From old English Dale meaning valley, or a Celtic name meaning attender at meetings. Also a common surname. A variant of Daly and Daley.

Dana
(Day-na)
From Denmark. Dana is associated with power and generosity. Dana was also the Celtic goddess of fertility.

Demelza
(Dem-el-za)
Fort on the hill. Demelza is of Cornish origin.

Elara
(Eh-la-rah)
From the Alder trees. Alar is a Breton name derived from Germanic sources.

Erea
(Eh-ray-a)
From Ireland.

Erie
(Eh-ree)
From Ireland. See Erea.

Erin
(Air-in)
From Ireland. See Erea.

Erina
(Air-ee-na)
From Ireland. See Erea.

Fanch
(Fonsh)
From France. Fanch is thought to be a female form of the Breton boys' name Fransez.

Fódhla
(Foh-lah)
Gaelic name for Ireland and the mythological wife of the god Mac Cécht, one of three brothers who took it in turns to rule Ireland.

Franseza
(Fran-say-za)
French woman. This is the Breton

version of the English Frances
and French Françoise, of Italian
origin, from the names Firenze
and Francesca.

Gael

(Gale or Gay-el)
Also Gaela, meaning from
Ireland and joy in Middle
English. Originally used to
refer to the Highland Celts,
and also the legendary hero
from whom the Irish race took
its name. Gael is also used as a
boys' name.

Gladez

(Gla-dez)
Breton version of the Welsh
name Gladys, from the word
'gwlad', relating to country and
sovereignty and a variant of
Roman name Claudia.
A 7th-century saint and mother of
St Kado.

Glenys

(Glen-iss)
Welsh name meaning valley girl
or pure. See Glenda.

Iona

(Eye-oh-na)
Island.
In the 6th century, Irish
missionary St Columba reintro-
duced Christianity after the fall
of the Romans and founded a
Celtic monastery on the Scottish
Isle of Iona, located between
Ireland and Scotland. Derived
from the Old Norse word 'ey'
for island.

Laorans

(Law-rance)
Breton equivalent of the boys'
name Laurence, referring to
the Latin for someone from
Laurentum.

Lesley

(Less-lee or Lez-lee)
Holly garden. Lesley is derived
from the words 'leas celyn'.
Also used as a boys' name.

Leslie

(Less-lee or Lez-lee)
Holly garden. See Lesley.

Marella
(Ma-rell-a)
Shining sea. An English name of mixed origins, including Hebrew and Latin. A variant of Marelda, Mary and Muriel.

Marilla
(Ma-rill-a)
Shining sea. A variant of Muriel.

Meriel
(Mer-ee-al)
Shining sea. A variant of Muriel.

Meryl
(Mer-el or Merl)
Shining sea. A variant of Muriel.

Morgan
(Mor-gen)
Sea dweller. Derived from Old English and the Old Welsh name Morcant and words 'mor' for sea and 'cant' for circle. Morgan is also as a boys' name. In Arthurian legend the sorceress and jealous sister of Arthur was Morgain, renamed Morgen Le Fay by Geoffrey of Monmouth in the 12th century, now known as Morgan Le Fay.

Morgana
(Mor-gah-nah)
Sea dweller. Breton name for King Arthur's sister, once a saint in Brittany with her own feast day. See Morgan.

Morgance
(Mor-ganse)
Sea dweller. See Morgan.

Morgane
(Mor-gan)
Sea dweller. See Morgan.

Muireann
(Moo-eer-an)
White sea. Derived from the Gaelic words 'muir' for sea and 'fionn' for fair. In the 6th century, a fisherman caught Muireann the mermaid in Lough Neagh and took her to be baptized by St Comghall, and she became a real woman.

Muirenn
(Mur-in)
White sea. See Muireann, possibly also related to Morgan and a variant of Muirne.

Muirgheal

(Mur-el)

Shining sea. Derived from the Gaelic words 'muir' meaning sea and 'geal' meaning bright. The Irish form of the name Muriel.

Muriel

(Myur-ee-el)

Shining sea. A medieval English version of the Irish name Muirgel. See Meriel and Muirgheal.

Nevidd

(Nev-id)

Sacred place.

Nevitt

(Nev-it)

Sacred place. A variant of Nevidd.

Tara

(Tar-ah)

Crag, or from the Hill of Tara. Tara was the seat of the high kings of Ireland.

Teamhair

(Taw-hair)

Crag or hill, or prominent position. See Tara.

ROLES

The names in this chapter refer to a person's position in life, from nobles, to warriors to mariners. Any name that implies a purpose is included here.

Aibhilin
(Ave-leen)
A variant of the French name Aveline, from which we also get Evelyn. Aveline may originate from the Latin word 'avis', meaning bird, but the Celtic form, which includes the spelling Aibhlinn, means longed-for child.

Aibhlinn
(Ave-leen)
Longed-for child. See Aibhilin.

Alastrina
(A-las-tree-nah)
A feminine form of the Scottish Alastair, meaning defender of mankind.

Alastrine
(A-las-tree-nah)
Defender of mankind. See Alastrina.

Alastriona
(A-las-tree-nah)
Defender of mankind. See Alastrina.

Andreva
(Ahn-dra-vah)
Warrior.

Arela
(Ar-la)
An Irish name meaning oath, it can be interpreted as witness to the message of God.

Awena
(Ah-wen-a)
A Welsh name meaning muse, or poetic person.

Baibin
(Bah-been)
A Celtic equivalent of the Latin name Barbara, meaning foreign woman.

BOUDICCA THE WARRIOR QUEEN

This 1st-century queen of the Britons led her army into fierce battle against the mighty but unpopular Romans, who, following the death of Boudicca's husband, had not only taken over rule of the Iceni tribe, but had flogged Boudicca and raped her daughters. Despite her heroic command and initial success in the revolt against the empire, she was eventually defeated and was said to have committed suicide by poisoning herself, rather than face capture.

Benalban
(Ben-awl-ban)
Woman of Scotland.

Betrys
(Be-triss)
A Welsh name meaning one who voyages through life.

Boadicea
(Bo-diss-ee-a)
Triumph. Latinized name of the queen of the Iceni, who later also became known as Boudicca (Boo-di-ca), from the English word 'boud' meaning victory.

Boudicca
(Boo-di-ca)
Victorious. See Boadicea.

Brendana
(Bren-da-nah)
Princess. Brendana is a female form of Brendan, meaning prince.

Brina
(Bree-na)
Defender. Brina also has Slavic origins and can be a variant of Sabrina and Brianna. See Breena.

Brisen
(Bree-sen)
Queen, and the sorceress from Arthurian legend who drugged Lancelot so he would think Elaine was Guinevere, resulting in the birth of Galahad.

Caera
(Kare-a)
Friend, often beloved. Caera is derived from the Irish word 'cara' for friend and the Latin 'cara' for dear. This Gaelic name is also thought to mean sharp or spear-like.

Caireann
(Kar-ran)
Beloved friend. Caireann is a variant of Cairenn, the dark curly-haired mother of warrior legend Niall of the Nine Hostages. Also a variant of the boys' name Ciaran and girls'

names Karen and Karan. See Caera.

Cairistiona
(Kare-ist-yona)
Follower of Christ. Cairistiona is a Scottish variant of Christina and comes from the male Christian.

Cara
(Kar-a)
Friend. See Caera.

Caragh
(Keer-a)
Friend. See Caera.

Cathbodua
(Kah-bo-dwa)
Victorious warrior.

Ceridwen
(Keh-rid-wen)
Blessed song. Ceridwen is a Welsh name inspired by the Celtic goddess of poetry, derived from the word 'cerdd' for poetry and 'gwen' for fair. Caridwen was the mother of 6th-century Welsh poet hero Taliesin. Variants include Ceradwyn and Cerridwyn.

Coleen
(Kol-leen)
Irish for girl. This is a popular name in the USA and Australia to connect to Irish roots.

Colleen
(Kol-leen)
Irish for girl. See Coleen.

Cora
(Kor-ah)
Seething pool. Cora is derived from Scottish origins, but also from the old Greek 'kore', meaning maiden, and possibly a variant of Corinna.

Coventina
(Kov-en-tee-na)
Iconic Celtic water goddess, thought to be a nurturer, also worshipped in Spain and Gaul.

Crystyn
(Kris-tin)
Of English origin, meaning follower of Christ. See Cairistiona.

Damhnait
(Dav-nit)
Fawn.Damhnait was the wife of a famous Munster king, Aed Bennan.

Dearbhail
(Daer-vil)
A poet's daughter. In the 7th century, Dearbhail was said to mean daughter of Fal, the legendary name for Ireland. Another meaning is thought to be true desire. Spelt as Dearbhla, Dearbhal and Deirbhile, it is a variant of Dervla.

Dearbhorgaill
(Der-vor-gil-a)
Daughter of the god Forgall and the wife of Tigernan Ó Ruairc, king of Breifne – did she elope with Dermot, king of Leinster, or was she abducted? Dearbhorgaill is more commonly known as Helen of Ireland. Also Derbforgaill and Anglicized as Dervorgilla, daughter of a male descendant of Connor.

Dechtire
(Dek-tir-a)
Tenth child. Dechtire is derived from the word 'deich', meaning ten. A charioteer from Irish

mythology, Dechtire was the sister of Conchobhar and mother of hero Cu Chulainn by sun god Lugh, who had abducted her from her husband, turning her and her handmaidens into birds.

Deirdre
(Deer-drah)
Broken-hearted and sad.
Also thought to mean fearful and enraged. Deirdre is a tragic heroine from Irish mythology.

Delbchaem
(Del-eb-hime)
Pretty one.
In Celtic legend, Art, son of Conn of the Hundred Battles, faces a dangerous and monstrous journey to rescue Delbchaem and take her for his wife.

Deoch
(Docks)
Meaning unknown. Deoch was a mythical princess of Munster.

Domhnacha
(Doe-na-ha)
Dedicated to the Lord.

Donalda
(Don-al-da)
Ruler of the world. Donalda is a female equivalent of the Scottish Donald.

Donella
(Don-el-la)
Ruler of the world, or dark-haired elfin girl.

Elen
(Eh-len)
Nymph, or sun ray, shining light. Elen can be a variant of Helen. Elen was the sister of British leader Conan Meriadeg, who founded Brittany in the 5th century.

Epona
(Eh-poh-nah)
Breeder. Epona is derived from a Welsh word meaning breed.Epona was a French horse goddess.

Erwana
(Air-wah-nah)
Yew. Erwana is a variant of Yvonne, meaning yew and relating to an archer or youth.

Fianna
(Fee-na)
A name derived from the legendary tale of warrior Fionn Mac Cool, whose band of men were known as the Fianna.

Fingula
(Fing-oo-la)
Fair-shouldered and beautiful. See Fenella.

Gormflaith
(Gorom-la)
Famous princess or lady. Derived from the words 'gorm' meaning illustrious and 'flaith' for lady or princess. Also Anglicized as Barbara.

Gormla
(Gorm-la)
Famous princess or lady. See Gormflaith.

Gormlaith
(Gorm-lah)
Irish and Scottish name meaning famous princess or lady. See Gormflaith.

GORMLAITH, DIVORCEE EXTRAORDINAIRE

This legendary lady and powerful beauty went through four husbands and was famed for her irresistible charms. Irish king Brian Boru was her third husband, who left her when she sided with the Danes and became the wife of Olaf Cuaren, Viking leader of Dublin. She was also known as the Mother of Dublin. Her three sons, Sitric, Murdach and Donough, ruled Ireland after Boru's death.

GRÁINNE NI MHÁILLE : THE SEA QUEEN OF CONNAUGHT

Described as 'one of the most remarkable women in Irish history', Gráinne, also called Grace O'Malley, was a famous 16th-century sea captain and pirate, who cut off her hair and dressed as a boy to pursue her seafaring dream. Also known as Granuaile, the name was derived from her father and brothers' nickname for her, meaning bald Grace. She was married twice, widowed twice and sent to prison twice, fighting the Irish and English for her denied rights, yet condemned for piracy. She was finally pardoned by Queen Elizabeth and is celebrated in James Joyce's *Finnegans Wake*.

Gormley
(Gorm-lee)
Famous princess or lady. See Gormflaith.

Granuaile
(Gra-nya-wail)
Bald grace.
Granuaile was the nickname of a Pirate heroine.

Heilyn
(Hie-lynn)
Cup bearer. Once a boys' name but now more popular for girls.

Imogen
(Im-o-gen)
Maiden. Imogen is derived from the Gaelic word 'inghean', meaning daughter.

Irnan
(Eer-nan)
Sword warrior. Possibly derived
from the Gaelic word for iron,
Irnan was an Irish goddess,
daughter of Conaran and sword
warrior for De Danaan.

Jocelyn
(Jaws-lin or Joss-lin)
Little Goth. Jocelyn is derived
from Old French for the
Germanic Gauts tribe.
Also used as a boys' name in
France.

Joyce
(Joice)
Warrior or noble. A Latinized
female variant of the Norman
boys' names Jodoc and Josse,
meaning warrior and lord.

Judwara
(Jood-wara)
Ruler or noble.

Kady
(K-dee)
English and Irish name meaning
first child, derived from the word
'ceadach' for first.

Loeiza
(Loh-ay-zah)
Renowned warrior. A Breton
variant of Louisa.

Macha
(Moh-hah)
Plain, or lost in the mists of time.

Meredith
(Meh-reh-dith)
A name of Welsh origin, meaning
great or sea lord.
Meredith is also used as a boys'
name.

Monca
(Mon-ca)
Wise counsellor.

Morrigan
(Mor-ee-gan)
From the Irish 'Mór Ríoghain'
meaning great queen.
Morrigan was a war goddess
in Irish mythology, who often
appeared as a crow.

Morwenna
(Mor-wenna)
A Cornish saint name derived
from the Welsh word 'morwyn',

meaning maiden. Morwenna also relates to a sea wave.

Neala

(Nee-la)

An Irish name meaning ruler or female champion, also associated with cloud. Neala is the female version of boys' names Neal and Neil. Also spelt Neila.

Nealie

(Nee-lee)

Ruler or female champion. See Neala.

Nerys

(Neh-riss)

Noble woman, or white lady. Nerys is of Welsh origin, derived from the word 'ner', meaning lord, with the feminine suffix 'ys'. It can also be an abbreviation of the old name Generys, which means white lady.

Noni

(No-nee)

Ninth. Noni is a name with Latin origins, and possibly a variant of Ione or Nora.

Rhian

(Ree-an)

Maiden. Also a variant of Rhiana.

Rhiannon

(Ree-an-on)

Great queen or goddess. Rhiannon is a modern form of the old Welsh name Rigantona.

Rivanon

(Ree-wan-on)

Great queen or goddess. A Breton variant of the Welsh name Rhiannon. Rivanon was the mother of Breton St Hervé.

Riwanon

(Ree-wan-on)

Great queen or goddess. See Rivanon.

Rosmerta

(Roz-mer-tah)

Great provider. Rosmerta is an Irish name of Gaulish origin. Rosmerta was a goddess of fertility and abundance.

RHIANNON THE DAUGHTER OF HEFEYDD

In Welsh mythology, Rhiannon was the daughter of Hefeydd, the first king of Dyfed. She was set to marry the horrible Gwawl, but Rhiannon had plans of her own and was in love with Pwyll. Their marriage was prevented by Gwawl, who cursed Rhiannon with infertility. But Pwyll, dressed as a beggar, managed to dispose of Gwawl, marry Rhiannon and conceive a child.

Ryanne
(Rye-an)
Little queen. Ryanne is the female form of Ryan.

Seva
(Say-vah)
A Breton name thought to mean peace. Saint Seva was a 6th-century saint from Brittany, where the parish of Sainte-Seve is dedicated to her.

Seve
(Say-vah)
Peace. See Seva.

Shanley
(Shan-lee)
Hero, or daughter of an old warrior.

Sheelagh
(Shee-la)
Sixth child. Sheelagh is derived from the Old Welsh word 'seissylt', meaning sixth. It is also related to the Latin Celia and Cecilia.

Sibeal
(Shib-ale)
Oracle. Sibeal is derived from Greek name Sybil.

Tamsin

(Tam-zin)

A Cornish name meaning twin. A variant of the English name Thomasina, the female version of Thomas.

Wenna

(Wen-er)

Maiden or of the white sea. Wenna is an abbreviation of Morwenna, and also a Cornish variant of the Welsh Gwen.

BOYS' NAMES

INTRODUCTION

From Adair, the spear warrior, to Yestin, the righteous one, this section contains over 700 boys' names that are either of Celtic origin or have been widely adopted amongst Celtic peoples. A name like Dabhaidh, for example, which is the Gaelic form of the Hebrew David, is included because, while not necessarily having Celtic origins, it is a name used by the Celts.

The section is broken down into chapters, so that the names are categorized under Events, Personality Traits, Physical Features, Place Names and Roles. For example, a name like Aengus, meaning great strength, will be listed under Physical Features, while a name like Muircheartach, meaning seaman or sea warrior, comes under Roles.

Events

The names in this chapter relate to events and happenings,
both specific events, such as a famous battle or a legend, and
generic occurrences, like victory.

Bradan
(*Bray-dorn*)
Salmon. The bradan feasa –
the salmon of knowledge – is
a central character in the legend
of Fion Mac Cool.

Bredon
(*Bray-dun*)
Salmon. A variant of Bradan.

Budoc
(Boo-dock)

BRADAN FEASA: THE SALMON OF KNOWLEDGE

According to Irish legend, when the Earth was created, all the knowledge in the universe lay in nine hazel trees that surrounded a well. Within the well lived a salmon, which fed off the hazel nuts that dropped from the trees, and thus acquired all the knowledge for itself. Whoever would eat the salmon would in turn acquire all the knowledge in the universe. That privilege fell to Fionn Mac Cool, who inadvertently imbibed some of the salmon while cooking it for his master, the poet Finnegas. And thus Fionn became all knowing.

Victory. St Budoc was the son of Azenor, who carried him while adrift in a barrel at sea (see Azenor in Girls' Names). He became a patron saint of Cornwall, Devon and Brittany.

Calatin
(Ka-la-tin)
Trial or hardship. Calatin was the name of an Irish warrior who served Queen Medb and was an enemy of Cu Chulainn.

Cathbad
(Kah-bud)
Battle.

Corentin
(Kor-en-tin)
A Breton name meaning hurricane.

Drust
(Droost)
Riot or tumult.

Drustan
(Droostan)
Riot or tumult. Drustan is a forerunner of the name Tristan.

Emmet
(Eh-met)
An Irish name bestowed in tribute to the rebel leader Robert Emmet.

Garvey
(Gar-vee)
Rough peace, or little rough one.

Kado
(Kar-doe)
Battle. Kado is a Breton word with its origins in the Welsh 'cad', meaning battle.

Kane
(Kain)
Little battle, or ancient, or beautiful. Kane has origins in different sources. In association with the name Keyne, it means little battle, as a variant of Cian it means ancient one, while it also has Welsh origins, meaning beautiful.

Neacal
(Nee-kul)
Victory of the people. A Scottish name derived from the Greek, a variant of Nicholas.

TRISTAN AND ISOLDE

Tristan was a Cornish knight, who was sent to Ireland to bring back a princess, Isolde (or Iseult), for his king, Mark of Cornwall. But on the way, Tristan and Isolde swallow a magic potion that makes them fall in love with each other. Though Isolde marries Mark, she carries on an adulterous affair with Tristan. There are many versions of this story with different endings, but the classic love triangle is thought to have influenced the Arthurian legend of Sir Lancelot and Guinevere.

Nedeleg

(Nay-de-lek)
Christmas. Nedeleg is a Breton form of the name Noel.

Nikolaz

(Ni-ko-lars)
Victory of the people. A Breton name derived from the Greek, a variant of Nicholas.

Nodhlag

(Nul-ig)
Christmas. Nollaig is an Irish form of Noel.

Nollaig

(Nul-ig)
Christmas. Nollaig is an Irish form of Noel.

Peredur

(Pe-red-er)
A Welsh name from Celtic mythology, Peredur was the son of Evrawg in the Mabinogion legends.

Tris

(Triss)
Tumult, din. Tris is an abbreviated form of Tristan.

Tristan
(Triss-tun)
Tumult, din. Tristan is derived
from the Celtic word 'drest'.
However, it is also associated with
the Latin 'tristis', meaning sad.
Tristan is a popular Celtic name,
inspired by the story of Tristan
and Isolde.

Tristen
(Triss-tun)
Tumult, din. See Tristan.

Tristian
(Triss-chun)
Tumult, din. A variant of Tristan.

Tristin
(Triss-tin)
Tumult, din. A variant of Tristan.

Tristram
(Triss-trum
Tumult, din. A variant of Tristan.

PERSONALITY TRAITS

The names in this chapter all have meanings that could describe a person's character. Meanings range from elements, such as fire, to animals, such as hounds or birds, and names in honour of gods and heroes, all of which bestow certain attributes upon the person bearing that name.

Adeon

(Ah-dee-on)

Derived from the Welsh 'adain', meaning wing, or Irish 'aodh', meaning fire.

Adwen

(Ad-wen)

Wing or fire. A Cornish variant of Adeon.

Aed

(Air)

A Scottish variant of the Irish Aodh, meaning fire. Aed is sometimes Anglicized to Hugh.

Aedan

(Ai-den)

Born of fire or little fire. A variant of Aodhan.

Aichear

(E-hir)

Sharp or fierce. Aichear was a famous musician in Irish legend.

Aidan

(Ay-den)

Born of fire. A variant of Aodhan, the diminutive form of Aodh, meaning fire.

St Aidan of Iona was a 17th-century monk who set up a monastery on Lindisfarne, from where he spread Christianity across the North of England.

Aiden

(Ay-den)

Born of fire. See Aidan.

147

Ailgenan
(Al-an-arn)
Mild or soft. Ailgenan was
the name of the 32nd king of
Munster. The name is often
written Algenan.

Aindreas
(An-dree-ahs)
Manly and brave. A Scottish
Gaelic form of Andrew.

Ainéislis
(An-esh-lish)
Careful, thoughtful.

Aneurin
(An-eye-rin)
A Welsh name meaning man of
honour – abbreviated to Nye.

Aodh
(Air)
Fire. An Irish name that gives rise
to variants such as Aidan.

Aodhan
(Eh-tharn)
From the fire, or little fire. A
diminutive form of Aodh.

Aodhgagan
(Ey-ga-gon)
Little fire. See Aodhan.

Arc'hantael
(Ark-shan-tel)
Shining nobility. A name derived
from the old Breton word for
silver.

Ardal
(Ar-dahl)
Great courage or valour.

Ardan
(Ar-dorn)
High hopes or high ambition.
Ardan can also mean tall man.

Arlan
(Or-lan)
Pledge or oath. Also a variant
of Arlen, meaning kind and
handsome.

Arlen
(Ar-len)
A name of Cornish origin
meaning kind and handsome.

THE LEGEND OF KING ARTHUR

The exploits of King Arthur are known throughout the world, and yet the truth behind this legendary king is shrouded in mystery. He is portrayed as a Celtic nobleman who lived in the Dark Ages, around the 5th century, and defended the Britain of the Romans and Celts against the invading Saxons. But the history of the time names no such king. So who was Arthur? A Welshman? A Cornishman? A Breton? Whoever he was – and it is likely that his legend was made up of the exploits of many different characters – he was undoubtedly a Celt.

Arlin
(Or-lin)
Pledge or oath. See Arlan.

Arlyn
(Or-lin)
Pledge or oath. See Arlan.

Art
(Art)
Champion or outstanding warrior. While Art can be short for Arthur, it is a Celtic name in its own right, with the same origin from a word meaning bear or rock, and thus applied to a strong and resilient fighter. Art was the name of a pagan king of Ireland who was said to go into battle with two angels hovering over him.

Artair
(Ar-tair)
Bear or rock. See Arthur.

Arte
(Ar-tee)
Bear or rock. See Arthur.

Arthfael
(Arth-fay-il)
Bear king. A Welsh name.

Arthur
(Ar-thur)
Bear or rock. Arthur is applied in the sense of strength or bravery, 'as strong as a bear'. Arthur is undoubtedly one of the most famous characters in Celtic mythology.

Artie
(Ar-tee)
Bear or rock. Diminutive of Arthur.

Artis
(Ar-tiss)
Bear or rock. Diminutive of Arthur.

Arto
(Ar-thur)
Bear or rock. Diminutive of Arthur.

Arty
(Ar-thur)
Bear or rock. Diminutive of Arthur.

Arzhel
(Ar-zel)
A Breton name meaning bear king. St Arzel was a 5th-century Welsh monk who founded a monastery in Brittany. He was believed to possess magic powers.

Arzhur
(Ar-zoor)
Bear. Another Breton variant of Arthur.

Balor
(Be-lor)
Dumbfounded. In Irish mythology, Balor was the one-eyed king of a giant race called the Fomorians. Whoever he looked upon with his eye was killed instantly, so he kept it closed most of the time.

Baruch
(Bah-ruke)
Spear thrower or blessed. Baruch

is a Hebrew name meaning blessed, but it is also a form of the Celtic name Bearach, meaning spear or marksman. See Bearach.

Baudwin
(Buh-dwin)
Brave friend.

Beathan
(Be-tharn)
A name of Scottish origin meaning life.

Bedivere
(Bed-i-veer)
Perfection. A variant of Bedwyr.

Bedwyr
(Baird-weir)
Perfection. In Arthurian legend, Bedwyr was one of Arthur's close companions. Variants include Beduir and Bedivere.

Beineon
(Ben-yone)
Benign or blessed.

Bernard
(Be-nard)
Brave bear.

Bernez
(Bayr-nez)
Brave bear. A Breton form of Bernard.

Berwin
(Bur-win)
Blessing.

Bladud
(Blad-oo)
Wolf lord. Bladud was a legendary Celtic king who supposedly founded the city of Bath in England.

Blaez
(Blaze)
An old Breton name meaning wolf.

Brassal
(Bra-sul)
Brave and strong. Brassal is more commonly an Irish surname, derived from the word 'bres', meaning courageous and strong in battle.

151

KING BLADUD AND THE FOUNDING OF BATH

According to the Celtic legend, Prince Bladud was a leper who was banished from the royal court because of his disease. He became a nomadic swineherd, and his pigs were all infected with leprosy too. One day he noticed his pigs wallowing in some hot springs and coming out cured, so he bathed in the springs himself and was also cured. He returned to his father's court and later became king, whereupon he built the city of Bath on the site of the springs.

Brastias
(Brass-tius)
Brave and strong. Brastias is a Cornish name. Sir Brastias was Uther Pendragon's bodyguard and one of the Knights of the Round Table.

Brazil
(Bra-sul)
Brave and strong. A derivation of Brassal, more commonly used as a surname.

Brennan
(Bren-an)
Teardrop or prince. Brennan is derived from the word 'braon', meaning teardrop, but can also be a derivation of Breanainn, meaning prince.

Bressal
(Bress-ul)
Brave and strong. See Brassal.

Brevalaer

(Bray-va-lair)
Black prince. Derived from the Breton words for raven and prince.

Briac

(Bree-ac)
Noble or strong. A Breton form of Brian.

Briag

(Bree-ag)
Noble or strong. A variant of Brian.

Briagenn

(Bree-ag-en)
Noble or strong. A variant of Brian.

Brian

(Bree-un)
Noble or strong.
Brian is one of the most popular names in Ireland, in memory of Brian Boru, a highly revered king of Ireland and founder of the O'Brien dynasty.

Briano

(Bree-ano)
Noble or strong. Variant of Brian.

Briant

(Bree-ant)
Noble or strong. Variant of Brian.

Briec

(Bree-ek)
Noble. Derived from Brian.
St Briec was a 5th-century Welsh monk who founded monasteries in Brittany.

Brien

(Bree-en)
Noble or strong. Variant of Brian.

Brion

(Bree-on)
Noble or strong. Variant of Brian.

Broc

(Brock)
Badger. The badger is an animal that appears often in Celtic mythology.

THE LIFE OF BRIAN

Brian Boru is one of the most important characters in Irish history. Legends portray him as a great warrior who united the clans of Ireland against the Norse invaders. One such battle, against the Dublin Norse and their allies from Leinster, which refused to be subjugated to Boru's rule, was fought at Clontarf on 23 April 1014 and it was here that Brian Boru met his end. However, he left a lasting legacy in the name of the clan O'Briain, which, with all its variants, remains one of the most common surnames in Ireland today.

Bryan

(Bry-an)
Noble or strong. Anglicized variant of Brian.

Bryant

(Bry-ant)
Noble or strong. Anglicized variant of Brian.

Bryon

(Bry-on)
Noble or strong. Anglicized variant of Brian.

Buadhach

(Boo-ark)
Victorious.

Caddell

(Ka-dell)
Brave, warlike or spirited in battle.

Cadell

(Ka-dell)
Brave, warlike or spirited in battle. A variant of Caddell.

Caradec
(Ka-ra-dek)
Beloved. A variant of the Welsh name Caradog.

Caradoc
(Ka-ra-dok)
Beloved. A variant of the Welsh name Caradog.

Caradog
(Ka-ra-dog)
Beloved. Derived from the word 'car', meaning love. Caradog, also known as Caratacus, was a British chieftain who fought against the Romans in the 1st century ad. He was also a Knight of the Round Table in Arthurian legend.

Caratacos
(Ka-ra-ta-kus)
Beloved. A Latinized form of Caradog.

Caratacus
(Ka-ra-ta-kus)
Beloved. A variant of Caratacos.

Carlin
(Kar-lin)
Little champion.
Carlin is also a girls' name.

Casey
(Kay-see)
Vigilant or watchful. Derived from the Irish 'cathasaigh'.

Cerwyn
(Ker-win)
A Welsh name meaning fair love.

Cledwin
(Kled-win)
Blessed sword.

Colm
(Kol-im)
Dove. Colm is a variant of Calum, derived from the Latin Columba.

Colman
(Kol-man)
Little dove. Colman is a diminutive form of Colm but has become a name in its own right, used by a large number of saints.

St Columba of Iona

St Columba, who gives his name to many Celtic names, such as Calum and Colm, was a learned Irish prince, who fell out with the abbott St Finian over a book to which he claimed ownership. A battle ensued in which many lives were lost, and Columba was exiled to the island of Iona in Scotland, where he set up a monastery and vowed to convert as many people to Christianity as had been killed in the battle.

Con

(Kawn)

High, wise and mighty, or dog keeper, or fleet-footed warrior. Con is derived from the word 'ceann', meaning head. In another sense it can be a diminutive form of Conaire, Conlaoch and Connal.

Conlan

(Kon-lun)

Prudent, wise, noble hero. A variant of Conlaoch.

Conlaoch

(Kon-lock)

Prudent, wise, noble hero. Conlaoch is an Irish name derived from 'conn', meaning chief, and 'laoch', meaning hero.

In Celtic mythology, Conlaoch's Well was the dwelling place of the Salmon of Knowledge (see Bradan).

Conn

(Kon)

Prudent, wise, noble hero or dog lover. A diminutive of Conlaoch and also Connal.

Conn was a high king of Ireland.

Conroy
(Kon-roy)
Hound of the plain. A variant of Conway.

Conway
(Kon-way)
Hound of the plain.

Cradawg
(Kra-dok)
Love. Cradawg is a variant of the Welsh name Caradog.

Cradock
(Kra-dok)
Love. Cradock is a variant of the Welsh name Caradog.

Cuinn
(Kwin)
Intelligent, wise. Cuinn is a variant of Quinn.

Dabhaidh
(Dav-id)
A Gaelic form of the biblical name David, which means beloved.

Dai
(Dye)
Beloved. A Welsh form of the biblical name David.

Daibheid
(Dah-ved)
Beloved. A variant of Dabhaidh.

Daibhi
(Dah-vee)
Beloved. A diminutive form of Daibheid.

Darby
(Dar-bee)
Free from envy. Darby is a derivation of Diarmaid.

Deaglan
(Dek-lan)
Full of goodness. Deaglan is derived from the words 'deagh', meaning good, and 'lan', meaning full. Its Anglicized form is Declan.

Dempsey
(Demp-see)
Proud one.

Deniel
(Dane-yel)
God has judged. A Breton form of the biblical name Daniel.

Dermot
(Der-mot)
Free from envy. Dermot is a variant of Dairmaid.

Devi
(Day-vee)
Beloved. Devi is a Breton form of David.

Diarmaid
(Dear-mid)
Without envy. Diarmaid is the origin of the name Dermot.

Diarmuid
(Dear-mid)
Without envy. A variant of Diarmaid.
In Irish mythology, Diarmuid was the nephew of Fionn Mac Cool.

Diwrnach
(Dew-er-nok)
Steadfast, unstinting.

Donnelly
(Don-a-lee)
Brave dark one.

Eanna
(Ay-ne)
Bird-like, or free as a bird. Eanna is a variant of Enda.

Eber
(Ee-ver)
Bow warrior. Eber is derived from the Irish Éibhear, and is a variant of the Welsh Ivor.

Edan
(E-dan)
Born of fire, or little fire. A variant of Aodhan.

Egan
(Ee-gan)
Born of fire, or little fire. A Welsh variant of Aodhan.

Elgin
(Ell-gin)
High-minded, noble. Elgin can also mean little Ireland, from the Gaelic 'Eilginn'.

Elidr
(Ell-i-dor)
Sorrow.

Elisud
(Ell-i-sood)
Kind, benevolent.

Ellis
(Ell-iss)
Kind, benevolent. A shortened
version of Elisud.

Elphin
Welsh Celtic boys' name
which is believed to
mean kind

Elwin
(Ell-win)
Noble friend.

Enda
(En-da)
Bird-like or free as a bird.
Enda is also a girls' name.

Eoghan
(O-win)
Born of yew, or youthful. A
forerunner of the name Owen.

Eoin
(Ee-yan)
God is gracious. Eoin is a form of
the biblical name John.

Erwan
(Air-wahn)
Yew, or youthful.
St Erwan was a 13th-century
cleric renowned for his fairness.
He became the patron saint of
lawyers.

Esras
(Ess-ras)
Empower.

Euan
(Yew-an)
Born of yew, youthful, or God is
gracious. Euan is a variant of the
Irish Eoghan, or of the biblical
name John.

Evan
(Yew-an)
Born of yew, youthful, or God is
gracious. Evan is a Welsh variant
of Euan.

Ewan
(Yew-an)
Born of yew, youthful, or God is gracious. Ewan is a variant of the Irish Eoghan, or of the biblical name John.

Fachtna
(Fark-na)
Hostile, angry.

Faolan
(Fway-larn)
Little wolf.

Farquhar
(Far-ker)
A Scottish name meaning friendly man or beloved man.

Farrel
(Fa-rul)
Man of valour. Farrel is an Anglicized form of the name Fearghal.

Fearghal
(Fur-gul)
Man of valour.

Feidhelm
(Fel-im)
Ever good. A shortened version of Feidhlimidh. Three kings of Munster were called Feidhelm.

Feidhlimidh
(Fel-i-mee)
Ever good. Feidhlimidh is an ancient Irish name. It could be associated with the word 'feile', meaning hospitable.

Felan
(Fee-lan)
Little wolf, or son of Faolan.

Felim
(Fel-im)
Ever good. An Anglicized form of Feidhelm.

Fergal
(Fur-gul)
Man of valour. An Anglicized form of Fearghal.

Gareth
(Gar-eth)
Gentle. Gareth is a Welsh name derived from Geraint.

Gareth was the nephew of King Arthur.

Gavin
(Ga-vin)
White hawk. A variant of Gawain.

Gawain
(Ga-wane)
White hawk. A variant of Gavin.

Geraint
(Gar-aint)
Gentle. Geraint is a variant of Gareth.

Gerwyn
(Ger-win)
A Welsh name meaning fair love.

Grady
(Gray-dee)
Noble or distinguished. Grady is derived from 'Grada', which was an old Irish term used to bestow dignity.

Gwencalon
(Gwen-kalon)
Shining heart, or bright-hearted. Gwencalon is an Old Breton name.

Haco
(Hay-co)
Flame or fire. Haco is possibly derived from the Irish 'aodh', meaning fire. Haco was a Cornish tribal leader.

Harvey
(Har-vee)
Worthy in battle. Harvey is a derivation of the French name Hervé.

Heddwyn
(Hed-win)
A Welsh name meaning fair peace, or holy peace.

Helori
(Ay-lo-ree)
Generous one. Helori is a Breton name derived from the word 'hael', meaning generous.

Hoel
(Ho-ul)
Eminent, conspicuous. Hoel is a Breton form of the Welsh name Hywel.

Hogan
(Ho-gun)
Youth, youthful one. Hogan is a variant of Hagan.

Hugh
(Hyoo)
Fire. Hugh is a modern form of the name Aodh, which means fire.

Hywel
(Hyoo-ul)
Eminent, conspicuous. A Welsh equivalent of the Breton Hoel.

Ith
(Ee)
A Welsh name meaning kindness or mercy.

Ithel
(Ee-thel)
Generous or merciful lord.

Kearney
(Keer-nee)
Warlike.

Kevan
(Ke-vun)
Gentle child, or well born. St Kevan was a 7th-century Irish saint who had a special bond with animals.

Kevin
(Ke-vin)
Gentle child, or well born. A variant of Kevan.

Liam
(Lee-um)
Wilful protector. Liam is a shortened version of the Germanic William, which is derived from 'wil', meaning will or desire, and 'helm', meaning helmet or protection.

Llew
(Hloo)
Radiant light, or leader, or lion-like. Llew is a diminutive form of the Welsh name Llewellyn.

Llewellyn
(Hloo-well-in)
Radiant light, or leader, or lion-like. Llewelyn the Great was a 13th-century ruler of Wales.

Lorcan
(Lor-kun)
Brave warrior. Lorcan is derived from the word 'lorc', meaning fierce. Lorcan is a name that crops up frequently in Irish history, as a saint's name, a king's name and the name of Brian Boru's grandfather.

Lughaidh
(Lew-ee)
Shining light, or oath. A variant of Lewis.

Maddox
(Mad-ox)
Beneficient, generous or fortunate. Maddox is of Welsh origin meaning son of Madoc, which means fortunate.

Madeg
(Mad-eg)
Beneficient, generous or fortunate. A variant of Maddox.

Manus
(Mar-nuss)
Great. Manus is derived from the Latin Magnus.

Marvin
(Mar-vin)
Eminent soul, or friend of the sea. The origins of Marvin could be a word meaning marrow or possibly brains, or alternatively the sea.

Menguy
(Main-gee)
Hound of rock. Menguy is a Breton name derived from 'men', meaning stone, and 'ki', meaning hound, wolf.

Mervin
(Mer-vin)
Eminent soul, or friend of the sea. See Marvin.

Mervyn
(Mer-vin)
Eminent soul, or friend of the sea. A variant of Mervin.

Morfran
(Mor-fran)
A Welsh name which means great crow.

Morvyn
(Mer-vin)
Eminent soul, or friend of the

sea, or great hill, or great fair one, or from the hill by the sea. A variant of Marvin or Morvan.

Mungo
(Mun-go)
Kind, gentle, dear. Mungo is mostly used in Wales and Scotland and is derived from the Welsh word 'mwyn'.
Saint Mungo was the nickname of Kentigern, the 6th-century saint who founded the Scottish city of Glasgow.

Naoise
(Nee-sha)
Meaning unknown.
In Celtic mythology, Naoise was the nephew of High King Conchobar. The name is now given to boys and girls.

Nechtan
(Neck-tan)
A Scottish name meaning pure.

Neese
(Neece)
Choice.

Ninian
(Nin-yun)
Origin unknown. The name Ninian is given in honour of a 5th-century saint.
Ninian Park was the former home ground of Cardiff City Football Club.

Nye
(Nigh)
Man of honour. A diminutive form of the Welsh name Aneurin.

Owen
(O-win)
Youth, born of the yew. Owen is a variant of Eoghan, meaning youth, or it could be derived from the Welsh 'oen', meaning lamb.

Padarn
(Pad-arn)
Fatherly, paternal. Padarn is a Latin name adopted by the Celts. Saint Padaran was a 6th-century cleric connected to King Arthur, who founded a church in Wales and was one of the seven founder saints of Brittany.

NAOISE AND DEIRDRE

Naoise was the nephew of Conchobar Mac Nessa, high king of Ulster, who was betrothed to Deirdre, the most beautiful woman in Ireland. But Deirdre and Naoise fell in love and ran away to Scotland. After several years, King Conchobar tricked them into coming back by promising to forgive them, but upon their return he killed Naoise. Rather than spending her life with Conchobar, Deirdre killed herself by throwing herself from his chariot, and was buried near Naoise's grave. A yew was planted on each grave and the two trees grew together and entwined.

Paol
(Pa-ool)
Humble or small. Paol is a Breton form of the Latin name Paul. Saint Paol Aurelian was a 6th-century Welsh cleric who became one of the seven founder saints of Brittany.

Phelan
(Fee-lun)
Little wolf. Phelan is derived from the Irish 'faol', meaning wolf, the 'an' making it a diminutive form.

Phelim
(Fail-im)
Constant or enduring goodness.

Piran
(Pi-ran)
Meaning unknown. Piran was a 5th-century monk and the patron saint of Cornish miners.

Pol
(Pol)
Humble or small. Pol is a Celtic form of the Latin name Paul.

Pwyll
(Pweel)
Steadiness.
Pwyll was the Lord of Annwn, the otherworld in Welsh mythology.

Quin
(Kwin)
Intelligent. A variant of Quinn.

Quinn
(Kwin)
Intelligent. Quinn is derived from the name Ceann and is more common as a surname.

Rafferty
(Raff-er-tee)
Rich, prosperous.

Raghallaigh
(Ra-hal-ee)
Valiant or brave.

Raibeart
(Ray-bert)
Bright famous one.

Rainbeart
(Ray-bert)
A Scottish name meaning bright famous one.

Reagan
(Ray-gan)
Furious, or impulsive. Reagan is derived from the Irish Riagan. Reagan is also a popular girls' name.

Reaghan
(Ray-gan)
Furious, or impulsive. See Reagan.

Regan
(Ray-gan)
Furious, or impulsive. See Reagan.

Reilly, Riley
(Rye-lee)
Outgoing people. Reilly was originally a surname, derived from the Irish Raghallach.

Riagán
(Ray-gan)
Furious, or impulsive.

Riobard

(Rob-aird)
Bright fame. Riobard is a variant
of Robert.

Roibeard

(Rob-aird)
Bright fame. Roibeard is a variant
of Robert.

Roibeart

(Rob-airt)
Bright fame. Roibeart is a variant
of Robert.

Ronan

(Ro-nan)
Little seal. Ronan is a diminutive
of the Irish 'ron', meaning seal.
St Ronan was a 6th-century
Irish missionary who worked in
Cornwall and Brittany.

Samzun

(Sarm-zoon)
Sun child. A Breton form of the
biblical name Samson. St Samzun
was 6th-century Welsh saint who
founded the abbey of Dol in
Brittany.

Seosamh

(Sho-sav or Sho-siv)
God shall add. Seosamh is an
Irish variant of Joseph.

Setanta

(Se-tan-ta)
The original name of the
legendary Cu Chulainn.

Shea

(Shay)
Hawk-like. Shea is derived from
the Irish Seaghdh.

Suibhne

(Siv-nay or Sigh-ve-nay)
Well-going.

Tanet

(Tar-net)
A Breton Celtic name that means
afire.

Tangi

(Tarn-gee)
Fire wolf. Tangi is a Breton name
derived from 'tan', meaning fire,
and 'ki', meaning wolf or hound.
St Tangi was a 6th-century Breton
monk.

Tanguy

(Tan-gee)

Fire wolf. Tanguy is a Welsh variant of the Breton Tangi.

Taran

(Tar-an)

Thunder or hill. Taran was the Celtic god of thunder, but the hill of Tara was also the legendary seat of the Irish kings, and so may have given rise to this name.

Uilliam

(Ool-yam)

(Lee-um)

Wilful protector. Uilliam is an Irish form of the Germanic William, which is derived from 'wil', meaning will or desire, and 'helm', meaning helmet or protection.

Uinseann

(In-shan)

Conquering. Uinseann is an Irish form of the name Vincent.

Visant

(Viss-on)

Conquering. Visant is a Breton form of the name Vincent.

Vychan

(Vi-kan)

Small. Vychan is a Welsh variant of Vaughan.

Weylyn

(Way-lin)

Son of the wolf, or the land by the road. Weylyn can be a variant of Waylon.

Yann

(Yarn)

God is gracious. Yann is a Cornish and Breton form of the biblical name John.

Yestin

(Yes-tin)

Just, righteous, fair. Yestin is the Welsh form of Justin.

PHYSICAL FEATURES

This chapter consists of names that describe a person's appearance or stature. In some cases this is implied by an object meaning, such as rampart.

Ael
(Ell)
Rampart. A name of Breton origin.

Aelhaeran
(Al-haran)
Iron brow. Aelhaeran is a Welsh name.

Aengus
(Eng-iss)
Great strength, or one choice. The origin of the name Aengus is open to interpretation. It is derived from the words 'aon' or 'óen', meaning one or prime, and 'gus', meaning either choice, or strength, vigour. Aengus was a god in Celtic mythology. Alternative spellings are Aonghus in modern Irish and Oengus in Old Irish.

Ailbe
(All-beh or Al-veh)
White, pure. Ailbe is a name used for boys and girls. In Irish legend, Ailbe was the daughter of Midir, the fairy king, and St Ailbe was a 6th-century monk from Co Tipperary, who blessed a barren river and made it abundant with fish. Churches were built in his honour at the five best fishing places along the river.

Ailbhe
(All-beh or Al-veh)
White, pure. See Ailbe.

Ailill
(Ay-lill)
Handsome, beautiful. Ailill is a legendary figure in Irish folklore and the name used to be extremely popular in Ireland.

ÆNGUS THE SWAN

A engus is the hero of many Celtic legends and was a deity of love and of youth. He is said to have had four songbirds flying about his head all the time, each one representing a kiss. In one story, Aengus falls in love with a girl he sees in a dream, and when he tracks her down he finds she has been turned into a swan. So Aengus turns himself into a swan and flies off with his lover, singing sweet and enchanting music as they go.

Ailin

(Ay-lin)
Handsome, beautiful. A variant of Ailill.

Alain

(Ah-len)
Handsome, cheerful or harmony. A Breton name that was introduced to England by a contingent of William the Conqueror's army. It has many variant spellings.

Alan

(Ah-lan)
Handsome, cheerful or harmony. See Alain.

Allan

(Ah-lan)
Handsome, cheerful or harmony. See Alain.

Allen

(Ah-lan)
Handsome, cheerful or harmony. See Alain.

ĀILILL ĀND THE CĀTTLE RĀID OF COOLEY

Ailill, son of Ross the Red, was married to Queen Medb of Connacht. They argued over whose cattle were the more valuable, and when Medb discovered that Ailill had amongst his herd a rare white bull, she set out to capture its equal, the Brown Bull of Cooley. Despite the heroic resistance of Cu Chulainn, her army succeeded in capturing the Brown Bull and taking it back to Connacht. But the jealousy between Ailill and Medb flared up again until he was chased out of the county and killed.

Allie
(Ah-lan)
Handsome, cheerful or harmony. Diminutive form of Alain or any of its variants.

Ally
(Ah-lan)
Handsome, cheerful or harmony. Diminutive form of Alain or any of its variants.

Alroy
(Al-roy)
Red-haired.

Alun
(Ah-lan)
Handsome, cheerful or harmony. See Alain.

Anarawad
(A-na-rod)
Eloquent or well spoken.

171

Anarawad is a Welsh name that was given to two kings in the 9th and 12th centuries.

Anghus
(An-gus)
Great strength, or one choice. See Aengus.

Angus
(An-gus)
Great strength, or one choice. See Aengus.

Angwyn
(Ang-win)
Very handsome or fair.

Auryn
(Aw-rin)
Golden one, in the sense of hair colour.

Banning
(Bann-ing)
Fair child or son of the fair one.

Beacan
(Bec-arn)
Small, little one.

Becan
(Bec-arn)
Small, little one. A variant spelling of Beacan.

Blaine
(Blayn)
From the word 'bla' meaning yellow, Blaine is a Scottish name meaning little yellow one, a reference to hair colour. It can also mean slender and may be a variant of Blane, the name of a 7th-century Scottish saint. Blaine is also a girls' name.

Blainey
(Blay-nee)
Little yellow one or slender. See Blaine.

Blane
(Blayn)
Little yellow one or slender. See Blaine.

Blayne
(Blayn)
Little yellow one or slender. See Blaine.

Blayney
(Blay-nee)
Little yellow one or slender. See Blaine.

Boden
(Bo-den)
Blonde.

Bodie
(Bo-dee)
Blonde. A diminutive form of Boden.

Body
(Bo-dee)
Blonde. A diminutive form of Boden.

Bowden
(Bo-den)
Blonde. A variant of Boden.

Bowdyn
(Bo-din)
Blonde. A variant of Boden.

Bowie
(Bo-wee)
Blond. Bowie is also a diminutive form of Bowen, meaning son of Owen.

Boyd
(Boid)
Fair haired. Boyd is a Scottish name derived from the Gaelic 'buidhe', meaning yellow or blond. It is also a surname and may be connected to the island of Bute, which is Bod in Gaelic.

Boyden
(Boy-den)
Blonde. In English Boyden means a messenger of victory.

Bran
(Brawn)
Raven. The name Bran is used for boys with very dark hair.

Brandan
(Bran-don)
Black raven or prince. As a derivation of 'bran', meaning raven, Brandan relates to appearance. But it is also a variant of Brendan, which means prince.

Brandubh
(Bran-duh)
Black raven.

Brann
(Brawn)
Raven. See Bran.

Brannoc
(Bra-nock)
Young raven. St Brannoc was a 6th-century monk who sailed from Wales to Devon in a stone coffin and founded a monastery at Braunton, where he is said to be buried.

Brannock
(Bra-nock)
Young raven. Variant of Brannoc.

Brarn
(Brawn)
Raven. Variant of Bran.

Brice
(Bryce)
A name of Welsh origin, meaning son of the ardent one or, from 'brych', meaning spotted or freckled.

Briciu
(Bric-roo)
Freckled. A Welsh variant of Brice.

Broin
(Bro-in)
Raven.

Bryce
(Bryce)
Freckled, or son of the ardent one. See Brice.

Cael
(Kay-ul))
Slender or thin.

Cahal
(Ka-harl)
Mighty in battle. Cahal is a variant of the Irish Cathal, derived from the word 'cath', meaning battle and 'val', meaning to rule.

Cahir
(Ka-harl)
Mighty in battle. A variant of Cahal.

Cailean
(Kai-lean)
Welp or puppy. Cailean is a Scottish name derived from the word 'coileán'. It is Anglicized as Colin.

Caley
(Kay-lee)
Slender or thin.

Calum
(Ka-lum)
Dove. Calum is derived from the
Latin name Columba, which means
dove. St Columba was a 6th-century
Irish missionary, and the name
Calum is often applied in tribute
to him, rather than for its literal
meaning.

Cameron
(Ka-mer-on)
Crooked nose. Cameron is
derived from the Celtic words
'cam', meaning crooked, and
'shron', meaning nose.
    Cameron is the name of a
famous Scottish clan and is
sometimes used as a girls' name.

Camey
(Ka-mee)
Crooked nose. A diminutive of
Cameron.

Campbell
(Kam-bull)
Crooked mouth. Campbell is
derived from the Celtic words
'cam', meaning crooked,
and 'beul', meaning mouth.
Campbell is the name of a
famous Scottish clan and is
sometimes used as a girls' name.

Canice
(Kuh-neece)
Handsome. Canice is derived
from Coinneach. St Canice, or
Cill Coinneach, was a 6th-century
Irish missionary who gave his
name to the town of Kilkenny.

Caoimhghin
(Qui-veen)
Beautiful at birth or comely
child. A variant of Kevin.

Caoimhin
(Kiv-een)
Beautiful at birth or comely
child. A variant of Caoimhghin.

Caolan
(Kway-lorn)
Slender. A variant of Caley.

Carrick
(Ka-rik)
Carrick is a name of Scottish origin meaning rock. It is a variant of Craig.

Cassidy
(Ka-si-dee)
The curly haired one. Cassidy is derived from the Irish surname O'Caiside, which means descendant of the curly haired one.

Cian
(Kee-in)
Ancient or long lasting. Cian is one of the most popular boys' names in Ireland, after the legendary Cian Mac Mael Muad, son-in-law of Brian Boru, who died with him at the Battle of Clontarf in 1014. The name gives rise to variants including Kane and Keane.

Ciar
(Kee-ar)
Dark one, or dark-haired one. Ciar is the male equivalent of Ciara.

Ciaran
(Kia-rorn)
Little dark one. Ciaran is a diminutive form of Ciar. Its variants include Kieran, Kieron and Keiran. Ciaran is a very popular saints' name.

Coinneach
(Ko-in-ock)
Handsome. Coinneach is an Irish variant of the Scottish and English Kenneth. St Coinneach was a 6th-century Irish missionary who gave his name to the town of Kilkenny.

Conal
(Kon-ul)
Hound, or high and mighty. A variant of Conall.

Conall
(Kon-ul)
Hound, or high and mighty. A name with links to both Con and Conaire. In Irish mythology, Conall Cearnach (Conall the Victorious) was the companion of Cu Chulainn, who avenged his death before nightfall. He is said to have been present

in Jerusalem as a prisoner of the Romans when Christ was crucified.

Conan
(Ko-narn)
Little hound or wolf. A diminutive form of Con.

Connal
(Korn-ul)
Mighty, or strong hound. Connal and its variants are associated with Conlaoch and can also be derived from the Gaelic 'cu', meaning hound or wolf.

Connall
(Korn-ul)
Mighty, or strong hound. A variant of Connal.

Connell
(Korn-ul)
Mighty, or strong hound. A variant of Connal.

Corcoran
(Kor-krun)
Reddened or ruddy, pertaining to hair colour.

Cronan
(Kron-arn)
Dark skinned, or little dark one. Cronan is derived from the word 'cron', meaning dark-skinned. St Cronan was a 7th-century Irish monk.

Cronin
(Kron-an)
Dark skinned, or little dark one. A variant of Cronan.

Cullan
(Kull-un)
Handsome lad.

Cullen
(Kull-un)
Handsome lad. A variant of Cullen.

Daire
(Di-ra)
Fruitful, fertile.
In Irish mythology, Daire Mac Fiachna was the owner of the Brown Bull of Cooley, which he refused to sell to Queen Medb, sparking the war between Ulster and Connacht.

Daithi

(Dah-hee)
Swift, nimble. Daithi was the last pagan king of Ireland, ruling from 405–426 AD.

Damán

(Da-varn)
Little stag, or tame. Daman is either derived from Damhan, meaning little stag, or from the Greek Damon, which means to tame or subdue.

Damhán

(Da-varn)
Little stag.

Daragh

(Dar-uh)
Like an oak tree.

Darcey

(Dar-see)
Dark. A variant of Darcy.

Darcy

(Dar-see)
Dark or descendant of the dark one. Darcy is derived from the surname O'Dorchaidhe. It is also a derivation of D'Arcy, meaning from the French town of Arcy. Darcy can also be a girl's name.

Daren

(Da-ren)
Little oak. A diminutive of Daragh.

Darragh

(Dar-uh)
Like an oak tree. A variant of Daragh.

Davin

(Dar-vin)
Little stag. A variant of Damhan.

Deiniol

(Dane-yol)
Attractive or charming. Also a Welsh form of the biblical name Daniel, which means God has judged.

Derry

(De-ree)
Like an oak. A variant of Daragh. Derry is the second largest city in Northern Ireland. It was originally known as Doire Colmcille, meaning the oak wood of Colmcille.

Dewain

(De-wane)
Little dark one.

Dillon

(Dill-on)
Streak of light, or faithful, loyal.
An Irish form of the Welsh name
Dylan.

Donagh

(Don-ah)
Brown-headed warrior. A variant
of Donncha. Donagh was the son
of Brian Boru.

Donn

(Don)
Brown or king. Donn was the
king of the underworld in Celtic
mythology, which is where the
meaning of king comes from.

Donncha

(Dun-a-ka)
Brown headed warrior. Donncha
is derived from the words 'donn',
meaning brown, and 'cath',
meaning battle. Donncha was the
son of Brian Boru.

Donovan

(Dun-a-varn)
Dark brown one or little dark
one. Donovan is derived from the
surname Donndubhán, meaning
son of the dark brown one. The
colour could refer to hair or eyes.

Dougal

(Doo-gul)
Dark stranger. A variant of
Doughal.

Dougan

(Doo-gun)
Dark one. A variant of Dugan.

Doughal

(Doo-gul)
Dark stranger. Doughal is derived
from 'dubh', meaning dark, and
'gall', meaning stranger.

Doyle

(Doil)
Dark stranger. A variant of
Doughal.

Duane

(Dwain)
Little dark one.

Dubhlainn
(Duv-lin)
Black challenger or black sword. Dubhlainn was a mythical character who wore an invisibility cloak in battle, given to him by the fairy queen Aoibhell.

Duff
(Duff)
Dark, or son of the dark one. An Anglicized form of 'dubh', meaning dark or black.

Duffey
(Duff-ee)
Dark, or son of the dark one. A variant of Duff.

Duffy
(Duff-ee)
Dark, or son of the dark one. A variant of Duff.

Dugald
(Doo-gald)
Dark stranger. A variant of Doughal.

Dugan
(Doo-gun)
Dark one.

Dughall
(Doo-gald)
Dark stranger. A variant of Doughal.

Duncan
(Dun-kun)
Celtic boys' name which is believed to mean either princely battle or (more likely) brown-haired warrior

Dunstan
(Dun-sten)
Brown stone.
   St Dunstan was Archbishop of Canterbury in the 10th century.

Dwayne
(Dwain)
Little dark one. A variant of Duane.

Dylan
(Dill-an)
Streak of light, or faithful, loyal. A Welsh form of the Irish name Dillon.

Ea
(Ay-a)
Fire.

Eirnin
(Air-nin)
Iron. A variant of Ernan.
Eirnin is an Irish saint's name.

Emrys
(Em-riss)
Immortal. Emrys is a Welsh name
derived from the Greek Ambrose.

Ernan
(Er-narn)
Iron.

Eurwyn
(You-win)
A Welsh name meaning gold and
white, or fair like gold.

Fearghus
(Fur-gus)
Strong man. Fearghus is the
origin of the Anglicized name
Fergus. Fearghus was a king
of Ulster.

Fergus
(Fur-gus)
Strong man. An Anglicized form
of Fearghus.

Ferris
(Fe-riss)
Rock.

Fiachna
(Feek-na)
Raven. Fiachna is derived from
the word 'fiach', meaning raven.

Fiachra
(Feek-ra)
Raven. A variant of Fiachna,
derived from the word for a raven.
In Celtic mythology, Fiachra was
turned into a swan for 900 years.
Fiachra is also a saint's name.

Finan
(Fin-un)
Little white or fair one. Finan is a
variant of Finnian, both of which
are diminutives of the name
Finn, which means white.

Finbar
(Fin-bar)
Fair-haired. Derived from 'finn',
meaning white.
Finbar was a 6th-century saint,
credited with driving a giant
serpent out of Cork.

Findlay

(Fin-dlee)
A popular Scottish name meaning fair-haired warrior.

Finlay

(Fin-dlee)
A variant of Findlay.

Finn

(Fin)
Fair-headed. An Anglicized form of the name Fionn.

Finnbar

(Fin-bar)
Fair-haired. See Finbar.

Finnian

(Fin-un)
Little white or fair one. A variant of Finan.

Fintan

(Fin-tun)
Fiery white. Fintan is a derivative of Fiontan.

Fionn

(Fin)
Fair-headed. 'Finn', meaning white, is the stem of numerous Celtic names, generally used to described hair colour. Fionn Mac Cool is a major character in Irish mythology, who acquired all the wisom in the world by touching the Salmon of Knowledge and then sucking his thumb.

Fiontan

(Fin-tun)
Fiery white. Fiontan is derived from the words 'fionn', meaning white, and 'tine', meaning fire. Fiontan is a very common saints' name.

Flann

(Flan)
Red or ruddy. Flann is derived from the word 'floin', meaning ruddy.

Floyd

(Floid)
Grey-haired. Floyd is derived from the Welsh name Lloyd, which comes from the word 'llwyd', meaning grey.

Flynn

(Flan)
Red or ruddy. Flynn is a variant of Flann, also derived from the word 'floin', meaning ruddy.

Gabhan

(Gav-an)
White hawk. Gabhan is a Gaelic form of Gavin.

Galvin

(Gal-vin)
A sparrow, or brilliant white. Galvin is derived from different sources and can be a variant of the Welsh Gavin, meaning white hawk.

Gannon

(Gan-on)
Fair-skinned or fair-haired.

Gethin

(Geth-in)
Dark-skinned, swarthy. A name of Welsh origin.

Gilroy

(Gil-roy)
Descendant of the red-headed one, or servant of the king. As a name of Irish origin, the 'roy' in Gilroy is more likely to derive from the word for red, rather than the French 'roi', meaning king.

Gwyn

(Gwin)
White, fair, blessed or holy. Gwyn is the male form of the girls' name Gwen.

Gwynfor

(Gwin-fa)
White, fair, or blessed lord.

Kavan

(Ka-varn)
Handsome. A variant of Kevin.

Keane

(Keen)
Ancient one. A variant of Cian.

Keelan

(Kee-lun)
Slender one.
Keelan is the male equivalent of the girls' name Keelin.

Keir
(Keer)
Dark-skinned.

Kenneth
(Ken-eth)
Handsome and fiery. Kenneth is derived from the Celtic words 'caomh', meaning fair, and 'aodh', meaning fire.

Kerwin
(Ker-win)
Little black-haired one. A variant of Kirwin.

Kieran
(Kee-run)
Little dark one, or son of the dark one. Kieran is derived from Ciar, and is a variant of Ciaran.

Kieron
(Kee-run)
Little dark one, or son of the dark one. A variant of Kieran.

Kirwin
(Ker-win)
Little black-haired one or son of the black-haired one.

Labhras
(Lav-ras)
Laurel (as in the shrub). Labhras is a variant of Laurence.

Lachtna
(Lokt-na)
The colour of milk. Lachtna was the brother of Brian Boru.

Lleufer
(Hloo-fer)
A Welsh name meaning splendour.

Lloyd
(Hloid)
Grey-haired one. Lloyd is derived from the Welsh 'llwyd', meaning grey.

Lugh
(Loo)
Shining light, or oath. A shortened form of Lughaidh.

Odhran
(Oer-an)
Pale, dun-coloured, sallow. Odhran is derived from the word 'odhar', meaning dun-coloured, sallow. Odhran is

a popular saints' name, and was the name of St Patrick's charioteer.

Oengus
(Eng-iss)
Great strength, or one choice. A variant of Aengus.

Oisin
(Ush-een)
Little deer.
A very popular Irish name, after Oisin, the son of Fionn Mac Cool, in Irish mythology.

Oran
(Or-an)
Pale, dun-coloured, sallow. A variant of Odhran.

Orin
(Or-an)
Pale, dun-coloured, sallow. A variant of Odhran.

Peadair
(Pad-ar)
Rock. Peadair is an Irish Celtic form of the biblical name Peter, which comes from the Greek 'petros', meaning rock.

Pearce
(Pierce)
Rock. Pearce is derived from the French name Piers, which itself is a form of Peter, meaning rock.

Pearse
(Pierce)
Rock. See Pearce.

Pedair
(Pad-ar)
Rock. See Peadair.

Pedr
(Ped-er)
Rock. Pedr is a Welsh form of the name Peter, which comes from the Greek for rock.

Penwyn
(Pen-win)
White head, or fair-headed one.

Per
(Pair)
Rock. Per is a Breton form of Pierre, or Peter.

Petroc
(Pair)
Rock. Petroc is a Celtic form of the biblical name Peter, meaning rock.

Quilan
(Kwil-an)
Slender, athletic. A variant of Quinlan.

Quinlan
(Kwin-lan)
Slender, athletic. Quinlan is derived from the Irish Caoinlean, meaning slender or shapely.

Quinlivan
(Kwin-liv-an)
Slender, athletic. A variant of Quinlan.

Randal
(Ran-dul)
Wolf shield, or strong defender. Randal is derived from the German Randolph, which itself comes from the name Randwulf.

Rhydderch
(Rid-irk)
Reddish-brown. Rhydderch is a name given to describe hair colour, but has been Anglicized as Roderick, which means famous ruler.

Rogan
(Ro-gun)
Red-haired.

Rooney
(Roo-nee)
Little red-haired one.

Rowan
(Ro-an)
Little redhead.

Roy
(Roy)
Red-haired, or king. Roy as a Celtic name originates from the word 'ruadh', meaning red, but it has also become a form of the French word 'roi', king.

Rúadhán
(Roo-orn)
Little redhead. An older form of Rowan.

Ruairí
(Roo-ree)
Red king. An older form of Rory. Ruairí Ua Conchobair was the last high king of Ireland, who was forced off the throne in 1175. His name has been Anglicized to Rory O'Connor.

Seaghdh
(Shay)
Like a hawk.

Shanley
(Shan-lee)
Small and ancient, or old heroic warrior.

Sullivan
(Sull-i-van)
Black-eyed one. Sullivan is derived from the Irish Suileabhain.

Taliesin
(Tarl-ee-ess-in)
A Welsh name meaning shining brow.

Tearlach
(Tar-ler)
Strong, manly, or instigator.

Tearlach is a name with French origins, but it can also be derived from the Irish 'toirdhealb', which means prompting, instigating.

Tomas
(Toh-mass)
Twin. Tomas is a Celtic form of the biblical name Thomas.

Trahern
(Tra-hurn)
Strong as iron.

Turlach
(Tur-la)
Strong, manly, or instigator. A variant of Tearlach.

Turloch
(Tur-la)
Strong, manly, or instigator. A variant of Tearlach.

Turlough
(Tur-la)
Strong, manly, or instigator. A variant of Tearlach.

Vaughan
(Vorn)
Small, little one. Vaughn is

derived from the Welsh 'fychan', meaning small.

Vaughn
(Vorn)
Small, little one. See Vaughan.

Wynford
(Win-fud)

White, fair, or blessed lord. Wynford is a variant of the Welsh Gwynfor.

Wynne
(Win)
White, fair, blessed or holy. Wynne is a variant of the Welsh name Gwyn.

PLACES

This chapter features boys' names that are inspired by a place, landmark or natural feature. Many of these names would have originated as surnames, which were often derived from the place a person lived or came from.

Annan
(An-an)
Lives by the river.
Annan is more often seen as a surname.

Argyle
(Ar-guile)
Land of the Gaels. Argyle and its variants are more common as surnames.

Argyll
(Ar-guile)
Land of the Gaels. See Argyle.

Athol
(A-thul)
New Ireland.

Balfour
(Bal-four)
Pasture or grazing land. Balfour is also a surname and the name of a place in Scotland. It may have derived from a greeting: 'The blessings of God on the harvest.'

Banadel
(Ba-na-dell)
Holy hill. Banadel was a Welsh king.

Bastian
(Bast-yan)
A Breton form of Sebastian, which is a Greek name meaning man from Sebasta. Sebasta was a city in Asia Minor, whose name was associated with respect and veneration.

Blair
(Blayr)
A Scottish name meaning plain or field, it would have referred to people who came from the plain or from the field.

Blair is also a boys' name and a surname.

Boynton
(Boyn-ton)
From the town by the river Boyne. Boyne means white cow in Irish.

Branwell
(Bran-well)
A Cornish name meaning raven's well.

Brendt
(Brent)
Mount or hilltop.

Brent
(Brent)
Mount or hilltop. A variant of Brendt.

Brenten
(Bren-ten)
Mount or hilltop. A variant of Brendt.

Brentley
(Brent-lee)
Mount or hilltop. A variant of Brendt.

Brently
(Brent-lee)
Mount or hilltop. A variant of Brendt.

Brenton
(Bren-tun)
Mount or hilltop. A variant of Brendt.

Bret
(Bret)
A Breton.

Brett
(Bret)
A Breton.

Brin
(Brin)
Hill, or noble and strong. Brin could be a variant of the Welsh Bryn, meaning hill, or the Irish Brian, meaning noble and strong.

Brodie
(Bro-dee)
A Scottish name meaning rampart.

Bryn

(Brin)

A name of Welsh origin meaning hill.

Buchanan

(Boo-can-on)

House for the canon. Buchanan is a place in Scotland and the name was given to people from that place, usually as a surname.

Cabhan

(Kav-an)

Grassy hill or hollow. Cabhan is often Anglicized as Cavan. County Cavan is a county in the Irish province of Ulster.

Calder

(Karl-der)

From the turbulent stream. Calder comes from Northern England and Scotland and derives from the Welsh 'caled', meaning violent, and 'dwfr', meaning stream.

Calhoun

(Kal-hoon)

From the narrow woods.

Camden

(Kam-den)

A name of Scottish origin meaning winding valley. In Old English, Camden means enclosed valley.

Cardew

(Kar-dew)

From the black fort. See Carew.

Carew

(Ka-roo)

From the hill fort or descended from the dark one. Carew could have its origins in the Welsh 'caer rhiw', meaning hill fort, or in the Irish surname 'O Ciardha', 'Ciardha meaning dark one. Carew Castle is in Pembrokeshire, South Wales.

Carey

(Kair-ee)

From the hill fort or descended from the dark one. A variant of Carew. Carey can also be a girls' name.

Cary
(Kair-ee)
From the hill fort. A variant of
Carey.

Cavan
(Ka-van)
Grassy hill, or handsome. Cavan
is a variant of Cabhan, but is also
associated with the name Kevin
and its variants.

Clooney
(Kloo-nee)
From the meadow. A variant of
Cluny.

Cluny
(Kloo-nee)
From the meadow. Clooney is
derived from the Irish word
'cluain', meaning pasture.

Clyde
(Klide)
From the River Clyde, or heard
far away. The Clyde is a river in
Scotland, but the origin of its
name is not clear. Clyde may also
be derived from the Welsh Clwyd,
which is a river in Wales.

Condan
(Kon-darn)
Bold settlement. A variant of
Condon.

Condon
(Kon-dorn)
Bold settlement. A variant of
Condan.

Corey
(Kor-ee)
From the hollow.

Craig
(Kraig)
Rock or crag.

Cuchulainn
(Ko-holl-in)
Hound of Culann, or Hound of
Ulster. Hound of Culann is the
literal meaning of the name,
but the legendary character has
come to be known as the Hound
of Ulster. Cu Chulainn is a major
figure in Irish mythology.

Dacey
(Day-see)
From the south, or southerner.

CU CHULAINN THE HOUND OF ULSTER

The legendary hero Cu Chulainn earned his name after killing a vicious guard dog belonging to a smith named Culann, in self-defence. Out of remorse, he offered to take the dog's place, and so assumed the name. Cu Chulainn grew up to become a fearsome warrior, single-handedly tackling the army of Queen Medb in the Cattle Raid of Cooley at the age of 17. His ferocity on the battlefield was said to transform him into a kind of monster. When he was mortally wounded by a cursed spear thrown by Lugaid, son of Cu Roi, Cu Chulainn tied himself to a standing stone in order that he might die on his feet. This stone is said to be the one at Knockbridge in County Louth.

Dallas

(Dall-us)
A name of Scottish origin, meaning from the meadow.

Dalziel

(Dee-ell)
From the little field.

Denzel

(Den-zel)
Denzel is the name of a place in Cornwall. Its meaning is uncertain, but suggestions include fallow deer, fort and fertile land.

Desmond
(Des-mund)
One from Desmond. Desmond is an area of South Munster.

Douglas
(Dug-less)
From the dark river.

Dunmore
(Dun-moor)
From the fortress on the hill.

Ennis
(En-iss)
Island. A variant of the Scottish Innis.

Erskine
(Ur-skin)
From the high cliff, or from the verdant hill.
Erskine is the name of a place in Scotland.

Fransez
(Frarn-ses)
A Breton name meaning from France.

Glen
(Glen)
From the valley.
St Glen was a Breton saint.

Glendan
(Glen)
From the fortress in the valley. Glendan is derived from the words 'gleann', meaning valley or glen, and 'dun', meaning settlement or fortress.

Glendon
(Glen)
From the fortress in the valley. See Glendan.

Glyn
(Glin)
From the valley. A Welsh variant of Glen.

Glyndwr
(Glin-dower)
From the black valley.

Glynn
(Glin)
From the valley. See Glen.

Glynne
(Glin)
From the valley. See Glen.

Gordon
(Gor-dun)
From the great hill.

Guthrie
(Guth-ree)
From the windy place. Guthrie is a Scottish name, commonly a surname.

Hurley
(Hur-lee)
Child of the sea, or child of the tides.

Innes
(In-iss)
Isle, or from the island. Innes is a variant of the Scottish name Innis.

Inness
(In-iss)
Isle, or from the island. See Innes.

Innis
(In-iss)
Isle, or from the island. Innis is a Scottish name.

Irvin
(Er-vin)
Green river. Irvin is derived from the word 'afon', meaning river. It has many variant spellings.

Irving
(Er-vin)
Green river. See Irvin.

Irvyn
(Er-vin)
Green river. See Irvin.

Kai
(Kye)
Field of battle. Kye is a Welsh form of the Latin name Caius. Kai was one of the Knights of the Round Table. It is also a girls' name.

Keith
(Keeth)
Forest or windy place. Keith is derived from the same surname, which itself comes from the name of a place in Scotland, meaning forest.

Kelvin
(Kel-vin)
From the narrow river, or narrow water. Variants include Kelvan, Kelvyn and Kelwyn.

Kendall
(Ken-dul)
From the Kent river valley.

Kendrick
(Ken-drik)
Pinnacle or champion. Kendrick is derived from the Welsh surname Cynwrig, meaning high peak.

Kent
(Kent)
From the border or from the edge.
Kent is the name of a county in England, which was occupied by the Celtic Cantiaci tribe.

Lachlan
(Lak-lun)
From the land of the lakes or lochs. See Lochlan.

Lee
(Lee)
From the river, or the meadow. The River Lee runs through Cork in Ireland, while lee is an Old English word meaning meadow.

Leigh
(Lee)
From the river, or from the meadow. See Lee.

Leith
(Leeth)
Scottish for wide river or harbour.

Lesley
(Lez-lee)
Garden of holly. Lesley is derived from the words 'leas', meaning garden, and 'cuilinn', meaning holly.

Leslie
(Lez-lee)
Garden of holly. See Leslie.

Lincoln
(Lin-kun)
A name derived from the Welsh meaning the settlement by the pool.

Lir

(Lee-er)

The sea. Lir was the god of the sea in Irish mythology. In Welsh mythology he is known as Llyr.

Llyr

(Lee-er)

The sea. Llyr is the Welsh equivalent of the Irish Lir.

Lochlan

(Lok-lun)

From the land of the lakes or lochs. Lochlan is a variant of Lachlan. The name was originally bestowed on the Viking invaders whose homeland, Norway, was known as the land of the lochs.

Logan

(Lo-gun)

Little hollow or cove.

Merlin

(Mur-lin)

Hill by the sea, or sea fort. Merlin has its origins in the Welsh name Myrddyn, which itself comes from the words 'muir', meaning sea, and 'dun', meaning hill or fort.

In Arthurian legend, Merlin was the tutor of the young Arthur.

Moffat

(Moff-it)

From the long plain. The name Moffat comes from the Scottish town of that name, which is derived from 'magh', meaning plain, and 'fada, meaning long.

Moray

(Me-ray)

From the settlement by the sea, or mariner. Moray is a Scottish Celtic name that was originally a place name, meaning the settlement by the sea. But it is also used as an abbreviated form of the Scottish surname Muireadhach, meaning mariner.

Morcant

(Mor-cant)

From beside the sea, or circle by the sea, or great circle. Morcant is an ancient Welsh name, which gave rise to the name Morgan. The prefix 'mor' could mean sea or great, while 'cant' means edge or circle.

Morgan

(Mor-gan)

From beside the sea, or the circle by the sea, or born of the sea, or born great. The 'mor' in Morgan means sea or great, while the 'gan' is either derived from 'cant', meaning edge or circle (see Morcant), or from 'geni', which means born or bright one. Prince Morgan of Gwent was a 7th-century Welsh noble who gave his name to the county of Glamorgan (Gwlad Morgan). Morgan is also commonly used as a girls' name.

Morvan

(Mor-vun)

Great hill, or great fair one, or from the hill by the sea. Like other Celtic names beginning 'mor', Morvan could be derived from a word meaning sea, or from one meaning great.

Morven

(Mor-vun)

Great hill, or great fair one, or from the hill by the sea. See Morvan.

Moryn

(Moh-rin)

Live by the sea.

Murray

(Me-ray)

From the settlement by the sea, or mariner. A variant of Moray.

Nairn

(Nairn)

Lives by the alder trees, or from the River Nairn. Nairn is derived from the name of a river in Scotland, which owes its name to the alder trees that grow along it.

Newlin

(New-lin)

From the spring, or new pool. A variant of Newlyn.

Newlyn

(New-lin)

From the spring, or new pool. Newlyn is of Welsh origin. Newlyn is a town in Cornwall.

Oileabhear

(O-liv-a)

Olive tree, or relic. Oileabhear is the Irish Gaelic form of the name Oliver, which means olive tree, but it could also be derived from the Norse 'Oilibhear', which means relic.

Olier
(Ol-yay)
Olive tree. A Breton form of the name Oliver (Olivier in French).

Onilwyn
(On-ill-win)
A Welsh name meaning ash grove.

Pert
(Pert)
From the thicket.

Perth
(Perth)
Thicket. Perth is the name of a county in Scotland.

Proinsias
(Pron-shuss)
Frenchman. Proinsias is an Irish form of the name Francis.

Ramsey
(Ram-zee)
Ram's island, or raven island.

Rhydwyn
(Rid-win)
From the white ford.

Roddy
(Rod-ee)
From the island of reeds, or famous ruler. Roddy is an abbreviation of Rodney, which comes from Hroda's island, or of Roderick (see Rhodri).

Ross
(Ross)
From the headland. Ross comes from a surname, derived from the name of a place in Scotland.

Scott
(Skot)
One from Scotland.

Sinclair
(Sin-klair)
From Saint Clair. Sinclair is an abbreviated form of St Clair, a name given to people from the place of that name in France.

Torrance
(Toh-rants)
From the small hills. Torrance is a variant of Terence.

Torrey

(Tor-ee)

From the tower, or small hills, or thunder. Torrey can be a variant of the Irish Tara, or an abbreviation of Torrance. It can also be derived from the name of the Norse god of thunder, Thor.

Tory

(Tor-ee)

From the tower, or small hills, or thunder. See Torrey.

Trefor

(Tre-vor)

From the large settlement. Trefor is a Welsh name and a variant of Trevor.

Tremaine

(Tre-main)

From the settlement made of stone, or encircled by stone. The prefix 'Tre' or 'Tref' signifies a settlement or town.

Tremayne

(Tre-main)

From the settlement made of stone, or encircled by stone. See Tremaine.

Trevor

(Tre-vor)

From the large settlement. Trevor is a variant of Trefor.

Uaine

(Oon-ya)

From the verdant place. Uaine is an Irish name meaning green.

Varden

(Var-dun)

From the green hill. Varden is derived from Old French.

Vardon

(Var-dun)

From the green hill. See Varden.

Waylon

(Way-lon)

The land by the road, or son of the wolf. Waylon can be a variant of Weylyn.

Roles

The names in this section refer to a person's position in life, from nobles, to warriors to mariners. Any name that implies a purpose is included here.

Adair
(Ah-dair)
A name of Scottish origin meaning wealthy spear, or owner of a number of spears. An alternative meaning of Adair is from the ford near the oak trees. It can also be a girls' name.

Adhamh
(A-dam)
A Celtic version of the name Adam, meaning man of the earth.

Ainmire
(Ahn-meer)
Great lord.

Airell
(Ahr-ell)
Nobleman.

Alasdair
(Al-as-dare)
Defender of men. Alasdair is a Scottish form of Alexander. It spread from Scotland to Ireland and beyond, picking up numerous alternative spellings on its way.

Alastair
(Al-as-tare)
Defender of men. An Anglicized spelling of Alasdair.

Alusdar
(Al-us-dare)
Defender of men. See Alasdair.

Armanz
(Ar-monz)
A name of Breton origin meaning bearer of arms.

Auley
(Or-lee)
Descendant.

Baird
(Behrd)
A minstrel or poet. Baird is
a variant of the English word
'bard'.

Banier
(Ba-nee-er)
Flag-bearer.
Sir Banier was one of the Knights
of the Round Table.

Bard
(Bard)
A minstrel or poet.
A variant of Baird.

Barden
(Bar-dun)
A minstrel or poet.
A variant of Baird and Bard.

Bardon
(Bar-don)
A minstrel or poet.
A variant of Baird and Bard.

Barnaby
(Bar-na-bee)
Consoling son. Barnaby is a
derivation of Barinthus, which
was the name of a figure in Welsh
mythology, who drove a chariot
for the people in the Otherworld.

Barnaib
(Bar-nee)
Consoling son. See Barnaby.

Barra
(Buh-ra)
Marksman or spear thrower.
Barra is also used as a pet form
of Finbar, meaning fair headed.

Barris
(Bah-riss)
Marksman or spear thrower.
A variant of Barra.

Barry
(Ba-ree)
Marksman or spear thrower.
A variant of Barra.

Bartley
(Bart-lee)
Son of Talmai (the farmer).
Bartley is the Celtic form of the
Hebrew name Bartholemew. It
was also used as a derivation of
Parthalon, who allegedy brought
agriculture to Ireland in the
third millennium BC.

Bearach

(Ba-rark)
Marksman or spear thrower.
Bearach is also used as a girls'
name. It has variant forms such
as Barra and Barry.

Bevan

(Be-van)
Son of Evan. Bevan is a Welsh
name formed from Ap Evan,
'Ap' meaning son of. It has also
come to mean youthful, or young
soldier. Bevan is also sometimes
used as a girls' name.

Bevyn

(Be-vyn)
Young soldier. See Bevan.

Bowen

(Bo-win)
Son of Owen. Bowen is derived
from the Welsh Ap Owen, 'Ap'
meaning son of. It is taken to
mean son of the youthful one
(Owen meaning youthful) or
even small victorious one.

Bowyn

(Bo-win)
Son of Owen. See Bowen.

Breanainn

(Bre-neen)
Prince. Breanainn is an old Irish
name derived from the Welsh
for prince, and it is the origin
of Brendan and other modern
variants. It may be used in tribute
to St Breanainn, the patron saint
of travellers, who was a
6th-century monk and the hero
of an old Irish saga, or Immram,
in which he voyaged for seven
years in search of Paradise. This
has been interpreted by some
people to mean that
St Breanainn was the first
European to sail across the
Atlantic to America.

Breandan

(Bren-dorn)
Prince. A derivation of
Breanainn.

Brendan

(Bre-neen)
Prince. A modern derivation of
Breanainn.

Burgess

(Bur-jiss)
Citizen. Burgess is derived

from the German word 'burg', meaning a town.

Cadeyrn
(Ka-dairn)
Battle king or lord of battle. Cadeyrn is derived from the Welsh 'cad', meaning battle and 'teyrn', meaning king. Cad is the stem for a number of Welsh Celtic names.

Cadfael
(Kad-file)
War chieftain. See Cadeyrn.

Cadman
(Kad-man)
Fighter. See Cadeyrn.

Cadwallader
(Kad-wol-a-da)
Leader in battle. See Cadeyrn.

Cairbre
(Kair-ber)
Charioteer or strong man.

Canank
(Kan-ank)
Offer. Canank is a variant of the Cornish Kanack and the Welsh Cynog.

Car
(Kar)
Fighter.

Carbry
(Kar-bree)
Charioteer or strong man. A variant of Cairbre.

Carney
(Kar-nee)
Winner, or victorious warrior.

Carr
(Kar)
Fighter. A variant of Car.

Carranog
(Ka-ra-nog)
Winner, or victorious warrior. A Welsh variant of Carney.

Caswallan
(Kas-wol-awn)
Leader In battle. Caswallan, also spelt Caswallawn and Latinized to Cassivellaunus, was the deified leader of the British Cassivellauni tribe, who fought the invading Romans and was immortalized in Celtic legend.

Cathair
(Ka-thair)
Great warrior. A variant of Cathal.

Cathal
(Ka-hul)
Great warrior. Cathal was a very popular name in Ireland during the Middle Ages and is sometimes Anglicized to Charles. St Cathal was a 7th-century Irish cleric who was adopted as the patron saint of the Italian army during the First World War.

Cathaoir
(Ka-thair)
Great warrior. A variant of Cathal.

Cathmore
(Kah-mor)
Great warrior or great battle.

Cearbhall
(Kia-val)
Fierce warrior. Cearbhall derives from the word 'cearbh', meaning hacking, suggesting a violent warrior.

Cearul
(Kar-ul)
Fierce warrior. A variant of Cearbhall, the name gives rise to Carol and Carl.

Cecil
(Se-sul)
Sixth child.

Chad
(Chad)
Warrior or battle. Chad is a modern derivation of the Old English name Ceadda, which stems from the word 'cad', meaning battle or warrior. St Chad was a 7th-century English bishop.

Christie
(Kris-tee)
Bearer of Christ. Christie is a diminutive form of the name Christopher, which is derived from Latin. Christie is also a girls' name.

Cillian
(Kil-ee-an)
Churchman. Cillian probably derives from the world 'ceall',

meaning church. However, it
is also associated with the word
'ceallach', meaning war or strife.
Variants include Cillin, Killian
and Keelan. St Cillian was a
7th-century missionary to
Germany, who was beheaded.
He was the Bishop of Warzburg,
where he is still celebrated
each year with a festival called
Killianfest.

Cillín
(Kil-in)
Churchman. A variant of Cillian.

Clancy
(Klan-see)
Son of the red warrior.
Clancy originally meant son
of Flannchadh, Flannchadh
meaning red warrior, the red
probably referring to his hair.

Clearie
(Klee-ree)
Minstrel or scholar. A variant of
Cleary.

Cleary
(Klee-ree)
Minstrel or scholar. Derived from
the word 'cliareach', meaning
minstrel or learned one, Cleary is
a common Irish surname but also
used as a first name.

Coilin
(Koh-lin)
Little chieftain. Coilin is a
diminutive form of 'coll',
meaning chieftain.

Colla
(Kol-ah)
High chieftain.

Comhghall
(Ko-all)
Close relative. The literal meaning
of Comhghall is fellow hostage.

Conaire
(Kon-oo-er)
Dog keeper or lover of hounds.
Conaire is derived from the
words 'Cu', meaning dog, and
'chobar', meaning aid. It is a
variant of Conor.

Conchobar
(Cro-hoor)
Lover of hounds. Conchobar is
sometimes pronounced Connor.

Conchobar was the name of a character in Irish mythology, the uncle of Cu Chulainn, who was killed by a sling-shot that lodged in his head.

Cormac
(Kor-muk)
Impure son, or son of the black-haired one, or son of the charioteer. 'Cor' has associations with defilement, but also the words for charioteer and raven. 'Mac' means son of. Cormac Mac Airt was an ancient king of Ireland.

Cormack
(Kor-muk)
Impure son, or son of the black-haired one, or son of the charioteer. A variant of Cormac.

Cormick
(Kor-muk)
Impure son, or son of the black-haired one, or son of the charioteer. A variant of Cormac.

Culann
(Holl-in)
Smith.

Culann was the mythical smith in the legend of Cu Chulainn, from whom he got his name.

Curran
(Kuh-run)
Hero or champion.

Dagda
(Dag-dah)
Kindly god. In Irish mythology, Dagda was a leader of the deities known as the Tuatha Dé Danann.

Dalaigh
(Dah-lee)
Counsellor. Dalaigh is derived from the word 'dail', which is the name of the Irish Parliament.

Daley
(Day-lee)
Counsellor. A variant of Dalaigh.

Daly
(Day-lee)
Counsellor. A variant of Dalaigh.

Deimhne
(Dev-neh)
Proof or assurance.

KING CORMAC AND THE GOLD CUP

Cormac Mac Airt was ruler of Tara for 40 years in the 3rd century, his reign noted for the wisdom he derived from a gold cup given to him by the sea god Manannan Mac Lir. The gold cup was magical and would break in three if three lies were told over it. But three truths would make it whole again. With this cup, Cormac was able to make sound judgements. Upon his death the cup vanished.

Delaney
(De-lay-nee)
Black challenger. Delaney has become a first name from the surname, derived from Ó Dubhshláine, meaning descendant of the black challenger.

Devin
(De-vin)
Poet or gifted one, or little stag, or dark one. Devin means poet or gifted one, but can also be a form of Damhan, meaning little stag, or a derivation of 'dubh', meaning dark.

Domhnal
(Doh-nah)
Ruler of the world. A form of Donald.

Donal
(Don-uh)
Ruler of the world. A variant of Donagh.

Donald
(Don-uld)
Ruler of the world.

Donall

(Don-ul)

Ruler of the world.

A variant of Donagh.

Doran

(Dor-un)

Stranger or exile.

Driscol

(Driss-kul)

Interpreter or messenger.

A variant of Driscoll.

Driscoll

(Driss-kul)

Interpreter or messenger.

Driskell

(Driss-kul)

Interpreter or messenger.

A variant of Driscoll.

Eachann

(E-kan)

Lord of the horses.

Eamon

(Ay-mun)

Guardian of the riches. A Gaelic
form of the English Edmund.

Eamonn

(Ay-mun)

Guardian of the riches.

A variant of Eamon.

Edryd

(Ed-rud)

Restoration.

Eibhear

(Ee-ver)

Bow warrior.

In Celtic mythology, Eibhear is
the name of the two sons of Mil
who conquered Ireland.

Eideard

(Ee-did)

Guardian of the riches. A Gaelic
form of the French Edouard and
the English Edward.

Einion

(En-yun)

A Welsh name meaning anvil.

Emlyn

(Em-lin)

A Welsh name possibly derived
from the Latin Aemilius, and
meaning one who strives, or a rival.

Eochaidh
(Och-yee)
Horseman.

Ferdia
(Fer-dee-ah)
Man of God.
In Celtic mythology, Ferdia
was the foster brother of Cu
Chulainn.

Gallagher
(Gal-a-ha)
Foreign helper, or foreigner's
friend. Gallagher is derived from
the Irish name Galchobar.

Gearoid
(Ga-rode)
Spear carrier, or spear ruler.
Gearoid is an Irish form of the
name Gerald.

Gilchrist
(Gil-crist)
Servant of Christ. In many
names of Irish origin, the prefix
Gil means servant of. In other
cases, it just means person or
fellow.

Gilmore
(Gil-more)
Servant of Mary.

Govran
(Gove-ron)
A Breton name meaning smith.

Griffith
(Gri-fith)
Strong leader or prince. Griffith
is a common Welsh surname.

Gwenvael
(Gwen-yel)
A Breton name meaning holy
prince or shining chief.
Gwenyael was a Breton saint.

Hagen
(Har-gun)
Noble son or youthful one.

Herne
(Hurn)
Horse lord.

Iarlaith
(Ear-la)
Lord of the west.

THE DEATH OF FERDIA

Ferdia and Cu Chulainn were foster brothers and friends, but they found themselves on opposite sides during the battle between Connacht and Ulster, known as The Cattle Raid of Cooley. Obliged to fight each other, their duel lasted for four days, and each night they sent each other herbal remedies for the wounds they had inflicted on one another. On the last day, Ferdia wounded Cu Chulainn in the chest and he was forced to use his magic spear, Gae Bolga, and kill Ferdia. In his grief, the exhausted Cu Chulainn collapsed, saying, 'Why should I rise again now he that lies here has fallen by my hand?'

Ifor

(I-for)

Lord or bowman. Ifor is a Welsh name meaning lord, but is a variant of Ivor, which is derived from Old Norse and means archer or master of the bow.

Illtud

(Ill-tood)

A Welsh name meaning master of the many.

Iollan

(Yul-an)

One who worships a different god. In Irish mythology, Iollan was the son of King Fergus Mac Roth.

Iomhair

(Eye-va)

Bow warrior. An Irish form of the Old Norse name Ivor.

Jago

(Jay-go)

Supplanter. Jago is a Cornish form of the biblical name Jacob or James, similar to the Spanish equivalent, Iago.

Jarlath

(Yar-la)

Lord of the west. A variant of the Irish Iarlaith. St Jarlath was a 6th-century saint, closely associated with Galway in Ireland.

Joyce

(Joice)

Lord. Joyce is derived from the Breton Iudoc or Judoc, meaning Lord.

Judoc

(Yoo-dok)

Lord. Judoc is a Breton name that gave rise to the name Joyce.

Keaghan

(Kee-gun)

Descendant of the youthful one. Names beginning with 'K' are often derived from Mac surnames, in this case Mac Eoghan, Mac meaning descendant, Eoghan meaning youthful one.

Keary

(Keer-ee)

Descendent of Ciar, or descendant of the dark one. A variant of Kerry.

Keegan

(Kee-gun)

Descendant of the youthful one. See Keaghan.

Kermit

(Ker-mit)

Son of Diarmaid, or without envy. Kermit is derived from the surname MacDiarmaid, Diarmaid meaning without envy.

Kerry

(Ke-ree)

Descendant of Ciar, or descendant of the dark one. A variant of Keary.

Killian
(Kill-ee-un)
Churchman, or war, strife.
See Cillian.

Laoghaire
(Lear-a)
Cow herd. Laoghaire is derived
from the Irish 'laogh', meaning
calf. Dun Laoghaire is the name
of a port on the Irish coast near
Dublin.

Lennán
(Len-arn)
Sweetheart.

Mabon
(Ma-bone)
A Welsh name meaning youth or
son.

Mac
(Mak)
Son of.

Mael
(Mwel)
Disciple, prince or chief.
St Mael was a 5th-century Breton
saint who lived in Wales.

Maeldun
(Mwel-don)
Disciple of the dark warrior.

Mainchin
(Man-kin)
Little monk. Mainchin is derived
from the word 'manach',
meaning monk.

Malachy
(Ma-la-kee)
Messenger of God, or servant
of St Sechnall. Malachy has two
possible derivations, one being
the Hebrew name Malachi,
meaning God's messenger, the
other being Maoilseachlainn,
from St Seachlainn or Sechnall.
St Malachi was the 12th-century
Bishop of Armagh. St Sechnall
was one of Saint Patrick's first
companions. Maoilseachlainn was
a high king of Ireland.

Malcolm
(Mal-kum)
Devotee of St Columba.
Mal means devotee or servant
and 'colm' is an abbreviation
of Columba.

Maoliosa
(Mwel-ee-sa)
Devotee of Jesus.

Marrec
(Mar-ek)
A Breton name meaning
horseman or knight.

Meilyr
(My-lure)
A Welsh name meaning head
leader or iron man.

Midhir
(Mi-dir)
Healer.
Sometimes spelt Midir, this
was the name of a Lord of the
Underworld in Irish mythology.

Molan
(Mo-lun)
Servant of the storm.

Muircheartach
(Mur-art-ak)
Seaman, or warrior from the
sea. Muircheartach is an Irish
name derived from the words
'muir', meaning sea and either
'ceardach', meaing skilled, or
'cath', meaning battle. It gave
rise to names including Murtagh
and Murdoch. Muircheartach was
the name of three high kings of
Ireland. Muircheartach Mac Neill
was an Irish military commander
of the 10th century.

Muireadach
(Mer-eek)
Seaman, or warrior from
the sea. A Scottish variant of
Muirchertach, which gave rise to
the names Murray and Moray.

Murdo
(Mer-dock)
Seaman, or warrior from the
sea. An abbreviated form of
Murdoch.

Murdoch
(Mer-dock)
A Scottish name meaning seaman
or warrior from the sea.

Murdock
(Mer-dock)
Seaman, or warrior from the sea.
A variant of Murdoch.

Murtagh
(Mer-ta)
Seaman, or warrior from the sea.
A derivation of Muircheartach.

Neal
(Neel)
Champion or passionate. Neal is
a variant of the Irish name Niall.

Neale
(Neel)
Champion or passionate.
See Niall.

Neall
(Neel)
Champion or passionate.
See Niall.

Nealon
(Neel-un)
Champion or passionate.
A variant of Neal.

Neil
(Neel)
Champion or passionate. Neil
is derived from the Irish name
Niall.

Neill
(Neel)
Champion or passionate.
See Niall.

Nell
(Neel)
Champion or passionate.
A pet form of Neil.

Nels
(Neel)
Champion or passionate.
A pet form of Neil.

Nelson
(Nel-sun)
Son of Neil, or son of the
champion.

Niall
(Nye-ul)
Champion or passionate. The
origin of the name Niall is
uncertain but it has taken on its
meaning by association with the
legendary King Niall of the Nine
Hostages. It may also have its
origin in the word 'nel', meaning
cloud.

MUIRCHEARTACH OF THE LEATHER CLOAKS

Muircheartach (or Murtagh) Mac Neill was a great Irish commander of the 10th century, who earned the nickname 'Muircheartach of the Leather Cloaks' after fitting out his army with rain-proof coats made of cowhide to keep them warm on their demanding winter expeditions. He won an important sea battle against the Vikings in Strangford Lough in 926, took Dublin from them in 939, sailed with a fleet to fight them in the Scottish Isles but was killed in combat at Ardee, near Clonkeen in Ireland, in 943.

Niallan
(Ny-lun)
Champion or passionate. A variant of Niall.

Nolan
(No-lun)
Descendant of Nualláin. Nualláin was a diminutive form of Nuall, which meant famous or champion.

Nuada
(Noo-ah-da)
Meaning unknown. Nuada is a god in Celtic mythology, the first leader of the divine race known as the Tuatha De Danann.

Nyle
(Nye-ul)
Champion or passionate. A variant of Niall.

Oscar
(Oss-ka)
Deer-lover. Oscar is derived from the Scottish Gaelic 'os', meaning deer, and 'cara', meaning love.

Oskar
(Oss-ka)
Deer-lover. See Oscar.

Owain
(O-ain)
Well born.

Paddy
(Pa-dee)
Noble born. Paddy is a diminutive form of Padraig or Patrick.

Padraic
(Paw-rik)
Noble born. Padraic is an Irish form of the name Patrick, which originates from the Latin word 'patricius', meaning of noble lineage. Padraic is the patron saint of Ireland.

Padraig
(Paw-rik)
Noble born. A variant of Padraic.

Padrig
(Pard-reek)
Noble born. A Breton form of the name Patrick.

Padruig
(Pad-rik)
Noble born. A Scottish form of the name Patrick.

Parthalan
(Por-ha-larn)
Son of the ploughman. Parthalan is an Irish Celtic form of the biblical name Bartholomew.

Powell
(Powl)
Son of Hywel. Powell is derived from the surname Ap Hywel, meaning son of Hywel, or son of the eminent one.

Pryderi
(Pri-dair-ee)
A Welsh name meaning caretaker.

Reamann
(Ray-man)
Advisor or protector. Reamann is an Irish variant of Raymond, which comes from the Germanic

NIALL OF THE NINE HOSTAGES

Niall was the last son of high king Eochaid Mugmedón. He had four half brothers, and in order to decide which of the brothers should succeed him, King Eochaid got a druid to set them some tasks. They were sent out hunting in the forest and came upon a hideous crone who guarded a well. Before she would let them drink from it, she insisted that they give her a kiss. All the brothers refused, except Niall, upon whose kiss the crone transformed into a beautiful woman, who granted him the sovereignty of Ireland.

'ragan' and 'mund', meaning counsellor.

Reamon
(Ray-mon)
Advisor or protector.
See Reamann.

Redmond
(Red-mund)
Advisor or protector. A variant of Reamann. Redmond O'Hanlon was a 17th-century outlaw, with

a band of followers known as Rapparees.

Rhain
(Rain)
Spear, or brave warrior. Rhain is a Welsh name whose literal meaning is spear, which implies a brave warrior.

Rhodri
(Rod-ree)
Famous ruler, or ruler of the

WHO WAS SAINT PATRICK?

Saint Patrick is believed to have been brought to Ireland as a slave from his native Britain in the late 4th century. Aged 16, he was put to work as a shepherd in Co Antrim, but after six years he had a vision telling him to convert his captors to Christianity. He escaped captivity and went to France to study to be a priest. Having achieved the status of Bishop, he returned to Ireland and spread the Christian faith. The legend that he drove all the snakes out of Ireland is probably symbolic, the snakes representing the pre-Christian pagans.

wheel. Rhodri is a Welsh name derived from the Germanic Roderick.

Rian

(Ree-an)
Little king. Rian is a variant of Ryan, derived from the Irish 'riogh', meaning king, with the diminutive suffix 'an'.

Riordan

(Rear-dun)
Royal poet. Riordan is an Irish name derived from 'ri', meaning king, and 'bardan', meaning poet.

Roarke

(Rork)
Champion or famous ruler. Roarke is a variant of Rourke.

Rory
(Ror-ee)
Red king or royal poet. Rory is derived from the gaelic 'ruadh' and 'ri', meaning red and king, but it is also used as a pet form of Riordan.

Ruairidh
(Roo-a-ree)
Red king. An older form of Rory.

Ruari
(Roo-ar-ee)
Red king. An older form of Rory.

Ryan
(Rye-an)
Little king. See Rian.

Sawyer
(Sor-yer)
One who saws wood. Sawyer derived from a common surname.

Scanlan
(Skan-lan)
Little trapper.

Scanlon
(Skan-lun)
Little trapper.
A variant of Scanlan.

Seamus
(Shay-mus)
Supplanter. Seamus is an Irish form of the biblical name Jacob, or James.

Sean
(Shorn)
God's gracious gift. Sean is a Celtic form of John and a very popular name in Ireland.

Semias
(Shay-mas)
Supplanter.
A variant of Seamus.

Seumas
(Shay-mas)
Supplanter.
A variant of Seamus.

Shane
(Shain)
God's gracious gift.
A variant of Sean.

Shaun
(Shorn)
God's gracious gift.
A variant of Sean.

Shawn
(Shorn)
God's gracious gift.
A variant of Sean.

Sheridan
(She-ri-dan)
Seeker, searcher. Sheridan is an
Anglicized form of Siridean.

Siridean
(She-ri-dan)
Seeker, searcher. Siridean is the
origin of the name Sheridan.

Sloan
(Slone)
Warrior, fighter.

Sloane
(Slone)
Warrior, fighter.
A variant of Sloan.

Somerlad
(Sum-er-lad)
Summer traveller. Somerlad is

a Scottish name derived from
Norse origins.

Somerled
(Sum-er-led)
A variant of Somerlad.

Somhairle
(Sor-lee)
Summer traveller, summer sailor.
An Irish form of Somerlad.

Sorley
(Sor-lee)
Summer traveller, summer sailor.
A Scottish variant of Somhairle.

Tadg
(Tige)
Poet. Tadhg Mor was a legendary
Irish chieftain who fell at the
Battle of Clontarf in 1014.

Tadhg
(Tige)
Poet. See Tadg.

Teaghue
(Teeg)
Poet, philosopher, bard.
A variant of Tadhg.

Teague
(Teeg)
Poet, philosopher, bard.
A variant of Tadhg.

Tiarnán
(Tia-norn)
Chief or lord of the household.

Tiernan
(Tia-nun)
Chief or lord of the household.
An anglicized form of Tiarnàn.

Tierney
(Tia-nee)
Chief or lord of the household.
A variant of Tiarnàn. St Tierney
of Clones was the godson of St
Brigid and later became Bishop
of Clogher in County Down,
Ireland.

Torin
(Tor-in)
Chief.

Tuathal
(Too-ul)
Leader of the people, or God's
gift. An Irish form of the Welsh
name Tudor.

Tudor
(Tyew-der)
Leader of the people, or God's
gift. Tudor comes from Old
Welsh meaning 'people mighty',
but is also a derivation of the
Greek Theodore, which means
gift of God.

Tudual
(Too-dwarl)
Leader of the people, or God's
gift. A Breton variant of Tudor.
St Tudual was a 6th-century
Welsh missionary to Brittany.

Tully
(Till-ee)
Leader of the people, or God's
gift. An abbreviation of the Irish
Tuathal.

Ultan
(Ult-en)
An Ulsterman. Ultan is a
common saints' name.

Urien
(Oo-ri-en)
Born into privilege.

CELTIC SURNAMES

INTRODUCTION

The original purpose of surnames was to provide an extra layer of identification wherever there might be confusion between two people with the same given name. If, for example, there were two Brians in your village, you might distinguish between them by referring to their trade, appearance or where they lived, e.g. Brian the charioteer, Brian with the red hair or Brian from the ford by the oak trees.

In Celtic culture it became commonplace to distinguish people by referring to their fathers, e.g. Donald's Brian and Dougall's Brian. In Wales they applied the prefix ap to mean son of, while in Ireland and Scotland they applied the prefix Mac for the same purpose, with the Irish also using O' to mean grandson or descendant of. The Welsh ap was subsequently contracted to just a p, or in some cases a b, to give us names like Price (son of Rhys) and Bowen (son of Owen). A similar contraction happened with Mac, whereby names like Mac Donald were shortened to McDonald.

Though these surnames had a hereditary basis, they tended not to last more than a couple of generations. The son of Donald Mac Kenzie (Donald son of Kenneth) would take the surname Mac Donald (son of Donald) and so on. However, this all changed about a thousand years ago, around the time of Brian Boru, the great Irish king. His grandson Teigue adopted his grandfather's name, giving himself the surname Ua Briain, now written as O'Brien. Such was Brian Boru's stature in Celtic folklore that the surname Ua Brien was maintained by Teigue's own descendants and thus the ubiquitous O'Brien surname spread.

Other prefixes that are common in Celtic surnames are Kil, Gil and Mul. Kil denotes a church, and so we can deduce that surnames beginning Kil refer to people from a place where stood a church. Gil is also related to the church, but stems from the Irish 'giolla' and the Scottish 'gille', which mean devotee or servant of. Gil is usually followed by a biblical name, such as Gilchrist (devotee of Christ) or Gilmore (devotee of Mary the Virgin).

The prefix Mul (sometimes altered to Mal) signifies a servant too, and again is used mostly in conjunction with religious icons. But Mul names can be confusing, because the prefix also stems from old Gaelic words meaning a hero, or a headland.

Just as the Irish Celts were getting used to the idea of their hereditary surnames, the Normans arrived and installed a few of their own. Well-known Irish surnames like Burke can be traced back to Norman roots (de Burgh in this case), while the common Irish prefix Fitz comes from the Norman method of denoting a son (fils).

Further confusion was added by the English, whose attempts to Anglicize Celtic surnames into something they could more easily recognize resulted in many names becoming mistranslated and thus their meaning lost. Anglicization also saw the Mac and O' prefix disposed of, so that many names like O'Sullivan and MacDuff became simply Sullivan, Duff etc. However, the last two hundred years have seen a lot of these prefixes restored.

In Wales, permanent hereditary surnames took longer to establish, possibly as late as the 1600s. There are relatively few Celtic surnames in use in Wales, exceptions being the likes of Glynn and Gwynn, Lloyd, Morgan and Vaughan, all of which are also used as first names, and those names like Price and Bowen that originally took the prefix ap.

Starting overleaf, I have listed 100 familiar surnames from Irish, Scottish and Welsh Celtic origins, together with their meanings. They tell us something of the land and culture as it was a thousand years ago and more.

Adair

From the ford by the oak trees. Adair is derived from 'ath', meaning ford, and 'darach', meaning place of oaks.

Allan

Allan has various spellings and different possible origins, including the Gaelic 'ailin', meaning rock, or 'aluinn', meaning handsome.

Avery

Avery is derived from the Old English Alfred, meaning elf counsel, and is also a modern form of 'Aimhrea', which means disagreement.

Bowen

Bowen is a contraction of the Welsh ap Owen, meaning son of Owen, with the p hardened to a b.

Boyd

Derived from the Gaelic 'buidhe', meaning yellow haired, or possibly a place name, in the Isle of Bute, or a river in England.

Boyle

A very common surname in Ireland, Boyle and O'Boyle are derived from the Gaelic Ó Baoghill, which

is thought to stem from the word 'geall', meaning promise.

Brodie

A Scottish surname denoting a place in Co Moray, whose name means ridge or brow.

Bruce

Originally a Norman name, thought to come from Brix in Normandy.

Buchanan

A place name in Stirlingshire, therefore, denoting a person from Buchanan.

Byrne

A variant of O'Broin, meaning a descendant of Bran. Bran means raven.

Calhoun

A corruption of Colquhoun, a place in Dumbartonshire, Scotland, whose name means the narrow woods.

Callaghan

A contraction of O'Ceallachán, meaning a descendant of the Munster king Ceallachán.

Cameron

A descriptive name for someone with a hooked nose, from 'cam', meaning crooked, and 'sron', meaning nose.

Campbell

Similar to Cameron, Campbell means crooked mouth, from 'cam' and 'beul', meaning mouth.

Cann

A contraction of McCann derived from 'ceann', meaning headland.

Carroll

The Carrolls are descendants of Cearbhaill, whose name comes from the Gaelic 'caerbh', for hacking, therefore implying a butcher or warrior.

Cassidy

A descriptive name, derived from the name Caiside, which means curly hair. The Cassidies are descendants of the curly-haired one.

Crawford

Crawford is a place name, meaning crow's ford, from the Old English 'crawa' for crow.

Craig

A Scottish surname derived from the Gaelic 'creag', meaning rock, which gave us the word 'crag' in English.

Daly

A contraction of O'Dalaigh, from Dalach, which was a name given to someone from the 'dail' (assembly or meeting place).

Dalziel

Pronounced Dee-ell, Dalziel comes from a place in Scotland, which takes its name from the words 'dal', meaning field, and 'gheail', meaning white.

Douglas

A Scottish place name, which comes from the Gaelic 'dubh' and 'glas', meaning black stream.

Doyle

From the Irish O'Dubhghaill, a clan name meaning descendant of the dark (or evil) stranger. The Scottish equivalent is Dougal.

Drake

The Gaelic origin of Drake is 'draca', meaning snake or monster, but the name could be taken from the contrasting English meaning of male duck.

Drummond

A name taken from a place in Scotland, which gets its name from the word 'druim', meaning a ridge.

Duff

Together with its variant Duffy, Duff is a Scottish and Irish surname that comes from the word 'dubh', which means black or dark.

Duncan

A descriptive name, derived from the old Celtic name Donnchad, which means brown warrior.

Dunne

This surname refers to somebody with brown hair or complexion, either from the Old English 'dunne', meaning dark or brown, or the Irish 'duinn', with the same meaning.

Edwards

A popular Welsh name, derived from the Old English 'ead', meaning wealth or prosperity, and 'weard', meaning a ward or guardian. The surname means son of Edward.

Ellis

Another popular Welsh name, meaning my god is the lord, Ellis (like Elliott) is a Celtic variant of the Hebrew Elijah.

Evans

The s at the end of names like Evans means son of, with Evan being an Anglicized form of Ifan, itself a variant of the biblical name John.

Farquhar

This interesting Scottish name comes from the Gaelic 'fear', meaning man, and 'car', meaning dear or beloved.

Farrell

This popular Irish surname is an Anglicized form of the Old Irish Fearghail, which means man of valour.

Ferguson

Not surprisingly this is a patronymic denoting a son of Fergus, which itself comes from the Gaelic 'Fearghus', meaning man of force.

Fitzgerald

A popular Irish surname with Norman origins, the prefix 'Fitz' derived from the French 'fils', meaning son of. Gerald is a name of Norse origins, which means spear ruler.

Flanagan

This common Irish name is derived from the old surname O'Flannagain, meaning descendant of the ruddy one, from the word 'flann', meaning ruddy.

Flynn

A corruption of O'Flann, a descendant of Flann, a name that means ruddy, as in complexion.

Forsythe

Forsythe has two possible origins, one being a place name, Fersith, which means mound of the fairies, the other being a descriptive name meaning man of peace or honour.

Fraser

This historic Scottish name is associated with the French word 'fraise', meaning strawberry, though that may not be its actual origin.

Gallagher

A name that can be spelt several ways, Gallagher comes from the Irish O'Gallchobhair, meaning descendant of the foreign helper.

Gilchrist

The prefix 'Gil' is a shortened form of 'gille', meaning a servant, so Gilchrist means a servant of Christ. The old Gaelic name for Christ was 'Criosed'.

Gillespie

In this case the 'Gil' prefix is assigned to the bishop, i.e. servant of the bishop.

Gilmore

A religious surname, Gilmore means servant of Mary, contrived of 'gil', meaning servant of, and 'more', a form of Mary.

Glynn

A surname taken from various places in Wales and Cornwall, Glynn stems from the Gaelic word 'glyn', meaning a valley. It is also a possible contraction of the Irish Mag Fhloinn, meaning son of the red one, as in red-haired or red-faced.

Gordon

A place-related surname, Gordon being a place in Berwickshire, Scotland, which was probably once the site of a large fort, 'gor' meaning large and 'dun' meaning fort.

Grant

The name of a Scottish clan that is derived from the French word 'grand', meaning large.

Griffin

A surname with several origins, through Welsh, Irish and Germanic, but all associated with dragons.

Griffiths

Derived from the Welsh name Gryffudd, which means strong leader, or leader with a strong grip, the 'gryff' element being associated with a dragon's claws.

Humphreys

An historic name with various spellings, Humphreys is derived from from the first name Humphrey, which means, paradoxically, peaceful bear.

Kavanagh

An Irish surname that can also be spelt with a C, Kavanagh is derived from the surname Coamhanach, which means mild, benevolent, friendly.

Kelly

The second most common surname in Ireland, Kelly comes from the surname O'Ceallaigh, meaning descendant of Ceallaigh, which means strife. It could also come from the old place name Kelli, in Devon, which comes from the local Celtic word celli, meaning a grove.

Kennedy

A famous irish surname, Kennedy is derived from O'Cinneide, which is contrived of 'ceann', meaning head, and 'eidigh', meaning ugly.

Kerr

A popular Scottish name with Norse origins, from 'kjarr', which became 'kerr' in Old English, and thus a place-related surname meaning bog or marshland.

Kilpatrick

A place-related Scottish surname, meaning from Patrick's church.

Kinnear

A place name in Fife, Scotland, Kinnear is derived from the Gaelic 'ceann', meaning head, and 'iar', meaning to the west.

Lennox

A district in Scotland, Lennox comes from the Gaelic name Leamhanach, which is made up of 'leamhan', meaning elm, and 'ach', meaning field. So Lennox was a field of elm trees, or by elm trees.

Lewis

A very old name that can be traced back to the old Frankish name Hludwig, which means famous battle.

Lloyd

A common Welsh surname derived from the word 'llwyd', which means grey, and, therefore, is applied to someone with grey hair.

Logan

And Irish and Scottish surname that can be derived from Irish roots, meaning descendant of the warrior, or from the Scottish place name, meaning hollow or lowland.

Lynch

An Irish surname that comes from the Gaelic Loingsigh, which means seaman, but is also a corruption of the Norman de Lench. Lynch, or Linch, is also an English name, derived from the Old English 'hlinc', meaning hill.

MacDonald

The most famous and populous of all the Scottish clans, the MacDonalds take their name from the descendants of chief Donald of the Isles.

Mackenzie

With the prefix Mac, meaning son of, Mackenzie and its alternative spelling mean son of Kenneth, and Kenneth means handsome and fiery.

Maguire

A contraction of Mag Uidhir, Mag is a variant of the prefix Mac, meaning son of, and 'uidhir' means dun-coloured.

Martin

Common in Ireland, Scotland and England, Martin is a religious name, an abbreviation of Gilmartin, which comes from the Gaelic 'gioll', meaning follower of, and St Martin.

McBride

A name found extensively in Scotland and Ireland, McBride is a contraction of Mac Giolla Brighde (Irish) or Mac Gille Brighde (Scottish), meaning son of the follower of St Bridget.

McCarthy

A contraction of Mac Carthaigh, from 'carthach', meaning loving.

McGrath

An Irish name meaning son of Graith, which means grace.

McIlroy

A contraction of Mac Giolla Ruaidh, 'giolla' meaning youth in this case and 'ruaidh' meaning red-haired, McIlroy and its numerous variants (including McElroy, MacGilroy etc) means son of the red-haired youth.

McIntosh

A common Scottish surname, McIntosh stems from the Gaelic word 'toisech', meaning leader, which has become Taoiseach in modern Gaelic and is the title given to the Irish prime minister.

McIntyre

A contraction of Mac and Saoir, which means son of the craftsman.

McKay

McKay and its variant McKee are derived from Mac Aodh, which stems from 'aed', the Gaelic word for fire.

Milne

A place-related name, common in Scotland, which refers to someone from a mill.

Moran

An Irish name that comes from the surnames O'Morain and O'Moghrain, both meaning descendant of the great one.

Morgan

A Welsh surname derived from the first name Morcant, which has several possible meanings, including born of the sea, or born great (see Morgan in boys' names).

Morrissey

An Irish surname that comes from the Gaelic name Muirgheasa, which is derived from 'muir', meaning sea, and 'geas', meaning action.

Munroe

A famous Scottish surname that could be a derivation of the Irish Munro, meaning from by the River Roe, or from the name Maolruadh, meaning tonsured redhead.

Murdoch

This Anglicized Scottish surname comes from the Gaelic Muireadhach, meaning a mariner or sea warrior.

Murphy

The most common name in Ireland, Murphy is a contraction of O Murchadha, which means sea warrior.

Murray

Generally regarded as a Scottish name, Murray has origins in Irish and English as well. The Scottish version comes from the Moray Firth, Moray meaning settlement by the sea. The English definition is from 'merry', while the Irish forms have two possible origins: Mac Muireadhaigh, meaning son of the mariner, and Mac Giolla Mhuire, meaning son of the follower of Mary.

Nolan

A contraction of O'Nuallain, from the Gaelic 'nuall', meaning shout, the original name probably referred to a crier.

O'Connor

A very popular Irish name, the O'Connors are descendants of Conchobhair, the famous king of Connacht.

O'Reilly

The O'Reillys are descendants of Ragheallach, who fought and died with Brian Boru at the battle of Clontarf, and was the great grandson of Maolmordha, king of Leinster.

O'Brien

The powerful O'Brien clan, originally O Briain, took its name from the great Irish king Brian Boru, who united Ireland against the Viking invaders.

O'Connell

This Irish surname is an Anglicized form of O'Conaill, from the first name Conall, which means hound of valour.

O'Neill

Another clan name, this time from the personal name Neil or Niall, which stem from the Gaelic 'niadh', which means champion.

O'Sullivan

The third most common surname in Ireland, O'Sullivan comes from Suileabhain, 'suil' meaning eye, but 'eabhain' being the subject of debate, some saying it comes from the word for hawk, others one, and others still dark.

Owen

A Welsh name taken directly from the first name, which means youth, or lamb.

Parry

An example of the contraction of the old Welsh naming form ap, meaning son of, followed by Harry, itself a pet form of Henry, which means home ruler.

Powell

A Welsh surname contracted from ap Hywel, son of Hywel, which means eminent one.

Price

A contraction of ap Rhys, meaning son of the ardent or enthusiastic one.

Pugh

From ap Hugh, son of Hugh, Pugh is a Welsh name built on Norman foundations, Hugh having come over in 1066, being an abbreviation of Germanic names like Hubert.

Quinn

The surname Quinn is an Anglicized form of O'Cuinn, from the Gaelic 'conn', meaning wise counsel.

Rees

A common Welsh name, Rees comes from the Celtic first name Rhys, meaning ardour.

Reid

The surname Reid and its many variant spellings (e.g. Read, Reed, etc.) has three possible origins. The first meaning is red, as in a person's hair colour or complexion. The other two are place-related, either from the Old English 'ried', meaning a clearing, or from the old word for reeds, denoting a river.

Ross

A surname related to numerous places in the British Isles, which take their meaning from a word meaning headland. In some cases it could also be derived from the Germanic 'hros', meaning horse.

Ryan

A contraction of the old Irish surname O'Maoilriain, the main part of which has two possible meanings, either chief of Rian or worshipper of Rian, Rian being a water god, or meaning little king, from 'ri', for king, and the diminutive 'an'.

Scott

Surprisingly, the origin of this surname does not denote a Scotsman but an Irishman. It comes from the word 'Scotti', which was a term used for Irish warriors who conquered the west of Scotland around the 5th century.

Stewart

This famous Scottish clan name, which became the ruling house in Scotland, is derived from the Old English 'stigweard', 'stig' meaning household and 'weard' meaning guardian. As well as the name Stewart, stigweard gave us the modern word steward.

Strachan

A surname taken from the Scottish place, originally known as Strathaen, in Kincardineshire, it could mean little valley or head of the valley, from 'strath', for valley, and 'an', for little, or 'ceann' for head.

Wallace

This famous Scottish surname actually has its origins further south, in England and Brittany. Derived from the Norman word 'waleis', meaning foreigner, it was applied mostly to Celts from the fringes of the Norman territories, such as Cornwall, Wales and Brittany.

CELTIC PLACE NAMES

INTRODUCTION

Some of the place names in the British Isles provide us with a clue to the migration of the Celtic people in the face of the Anglo-Saxon influx following the end of Roman rule. As the Saxons took over most of England, and the Celts withdrew to the western fringes, most former Celtic settlements, whose names had survived through the Roman occupation, were renamed or Anglicized beyond recognition.

However, throughout the areas of Europe that were once dominated by the Celts, there are still places whose names still bear the hallmarks of their Celtic history. Belgium, for example, is unmistakeably named after the Celtic Belgiae tribe. Likewise Paris, from the Parisii, and Kent, from the Cantiaci.

Rivers too still carry their Celtic roots from source to

sea. The Rhine, the Rhône, the Danube, the Thames, the Ouse, the Avon, the Severn: these major European rivers all take their names from Celtic origins. Indeed, rivers seem to have been less susceptible to name changes through history than towns. Perhaps it was considered ill-fated to tinker with something as sacred as a river.

To find consistent evidence of Celtic place names, you have to travel to the regions where the Celts continued to proliferate beyond the invasions of the Anglo-Saxons, the Vikings and the Normans; to Devon and Cornwall, to Brittany, Wales and Cumbria, to Scotland and, of course, to Ireland. Here you will come across repeated examples of prefixes that originate in Celtic words for generic topographical features, coupled with Celtic descriptive words, or determiners, that were applied to distinguish one hill, say, from another.

Watch out for these generic Celtic prefixes:

Aber
The mouth of a river, e.g. Aberga-venny in Wales (mouth of the river Gavenny) and Aberdeen in Scotland (mouth of the river Don).

Bally
A common prefix in Ireland, from the Gaelic 'baile', meaning a farmstead or village in Irish Gaelic. E.g. Ballygowan (MacGabhann's village).

Ben
From 'beinn', meaning a hill or mountain. E.g. Ben Nevis.

Car or Caer
From 'cair', meaning a fortified town. E.g. Carlisle (fortified town of Lugus, a god).

Combe, Cwm and Cum
All words for a valley, found in Devon, Cornwall and Wales. E.g. Ilfracombe and Cwmbran.

Dun, Don and Down
From the Gaelic 'don', meaning a fortified place. E.g. Dundalk (Dalgan's fortress), Donegal (fortress of the foreigners) and Downpatrick (Patrick's fortress).

Glen
From 'gleann', meaning a narrow valley. E.g. Glenfiddich in Scotland (valley of the river Fiddich).

Llan
A very common Welsh prefix meaning church. E.g. Llanelli (church of St Elli) and Llangollen (church of St Collen).

Pen

Commonly found in Cornwall, Wales and Cumbria, this comes from 'penn', meaning a hill, tor or headland. E.g. Penzance in Cornwall (holy headland) and Penrith in Cumbria (probably red hill).

Pol

A very distinctive Cornish place prefix, meaning pool. E.g. Polperro and Polzeath.

Tor

Meaning a tor, a rocky outcrop or hill, this is particularly common in Devon. E.g. Torquay and Torbay.

Tre or Tref

Common in Cornwall and Wales, this prefix means farmstead, and later came to denote a town. E.g. Tremellin (farm by a mill) and Trefechan (small farmstead).

These generic place names were attached to a determiner, with the generic preceding the determiner in most cases, i.e. hill of green, as opposed to green hill. An exception is combe, which for some reason tends to come second in most place names, possibly because it was adopted by the Anglo-Saxons – one of the few Celtic naming words that were – who tended to build their place names with the determiner first, followed by the generic, e.g. Oxford (ford for oxen).

The prize for the ultimate descriptive place name, which displays the full versatility of the Celtic linguistic tradition, is the famous Anglesey town of Llanfairpwllg-wyngyllgogerychwyrndrobwllllantysiliogogogoch, which expanded its name from Llanfair Pwllgwyngyll (St Mary's church in the hollow of the white hazel) in 1860, purely so it could claim to be the longest place name in the world. A triumph for the Celtic languages? Or just a faster way of saying, 'St Mary's Church in the hollow of the white hazel near the rapid whirlpool and the church of St Tysilio by the red cave'?

CELTIC NAMES LIVE ON

More than any other of the great peoples that held dominion over parts of Europe in the same era as the Celtic heyday, the Celtic identity has survived to the present day, and indeed is in the ascendancy. Why should this be? What was it about the Celts that makes their descendants – and even people who may not be their descendants – so proud of their Celtic roots?

Ireland remains the stronghold of Celtic heritage, maintaining Irish Gaelic as an official language, spoken by 20 per cent of the population and indeed spoken as the mother tongue in parts of the country. In Wales the Celtic language has enjoyed a significant revival, expanding from the more extreme corners where it was steadfastly preserved as the first language to now being taught in schools throughout the country, used on signs and for place names. There are Welsh language television channels and one place where you are bound to hear Welsh spoken freely is the Eisteddfod, that traditional celebration of culture, comprising singers, musicians, poets etc – all perpetuating the Celtic love of the creative arts.

The Celtic language of Scotland is not as widespread as its counterparts in Wales and Ireland, yet Scottish Gaelic is spoken by over 80,000 people living in the historical Celtic territories of the Highlands and Islands. Old Highland traditions are also very much a part of the modern Scottish identity: the Highland Games, famous for the strength contest of tossing the caber, Highland dancing, the bagpipes, the traditional Highland dress of tartan kilt, sporran and *Sgian Dubh* (hidden blade), the small knife tucked into the hose.

One of Scotland's two biggest football clubs is called Celtic, a name echoed in America by the Boston Celtics basketball club.

In Cornwall and Brittany, concerted efforts to preserve Celtic culture have seen an increase in interest for learning the old Celtic languages of Cornish and Breton, and Celtic cultural events are still keenly observed. Brittany maintains its Celtic traditions through its 'Pardons', which are Celtic celebrations with a religious element, and the town of Lorient hosts an annual festival, which attracts performers from throughout the Celtic world.

This is a good occasion to observe the cultural similarities that have bridged the gap between those Celtic parts of the British Isles, Brittany and the Celtic region of north-west Spain, consisting of Galicia and parts of Asturias. The dancing, the pipes, the dress are all clearly rooted in the same cultural ancestry. This Celtic part of Spain also has its own language, distinct from Spanish, and indeed there is a theory that the Irish Celts – who we know were distinct from those who migrated through England – originally came from Spain.

But what of England? Were the Celts so ruthlessly oppressed by the Anglo-Saxons that no vestige of Celticism remains in English culture? Not at all. The quintessentially English May Day celebrations stem from Celtic tradition, the Arthurian legend is kept alive in parts of the West Country, stoked by speculation as to the true location of Camelot, and that great Celtic queen, Boudicca, remains a proud symbol of English fortitude and independence.

However, a significant part of the Celtic identity lies in the opposition to English rule. The formation of the Welsh Assembly in 1998 and the Scottish Parliament in 1999 have seen a degree of political independence return to these Celtic homelands for the first time in hundreds of years, and the sense of independence is growing. This isn't just confined to Scotland and Wales either: everywhere in the world where Scottish and Welsh descendants have settled, they retain an active interest in the plight of their Celtic fatherlands, just as the Irish descendants throughout the world retain a strong sense of their Irish identity.

But why should this be? True, the sense of belonging to an oppressed minority is a strong unifying force, but there is more to being a Celt than just a political stance. The fact that the Celtic star is rising again after all these years has much to do with how these modern-day Celts want to perceive themselves. And the simple truth is, a Celtic identity is cool.

It speaks of art, of music, of poetry, literature and romance, of craftsmanship and beauty, of wit and ingenuity. Celtic has become a byword for non-conformity, creativity and passion. So to be a Celt today is to align yourself with these characteristics.

And yet how can you tell if you are a Celt? Such has been the mixture of cultures and races over the centuries, the names appropriated and misappropriated, that a man called O'Brien may well be of Anglo-Saxon, Viking or Norman descent, just as a man named Smith may well be a pure-blooded Celt. The obvious answer is that Celtic today is a state of mind, an alignment with a way of thinking, a set of values, that marks you out as an artist. It is a sense of belonging to a past, and yet that past is every bit as nebulous as the present. Perhaps this tells us something about the Celts themselves. We know they were not one tribe, one race, but a diverse set of peoples who shared certain characteristics and a language. It is those characteristics and that language that live on today, and perhaps if you regard yourself as a Celt, if somewhere deep inside yourself there is a desire to be a Celt, then who is to say you are not a Celt.

In years to come, perhaps science will discover that that Celtic yearning is some biological vestige, the manifestation of a piece of hereditary DNA passed down from generation to generation from the original Celtic source. Until that day comes, the best evidence we have that the Celts lived and thrived and instilled an influence that is still dominant today is the Celtic names that keep appearing amongst the artists, writers, musicians, innovators and warriors of the modern day.

Celtic names in literature

The Celtic love of storytelling continues today, with many Celtic names at the forefront of modern literature. Dublin has produced more Nobel Prize winners for literature than any other city, and the list of great Irish writers includes such famous name as James Joyce (from the Breton Iodoc, the name of a prince), Seamus Heaney (descendant of Éighneach) and George Bernard Shaw (Anglicized form of Sitheach, meaning wolf). They gave the world respectively *Ulysses*, *Death of a Naturalist* and *Pygmalion*, the play that became the musical *My Fair Lady*. Before them came the Irish poet and Celtic revivalist William Butler Yeats, whose surname stems from Old English, but became quite widespread in Ireland, via Scotland.

The Welsh poet Dylan Thomas ('Under Milk Wood', 'Do

Not Go Gentle Into That Good Night') has a biblical surname, but his first name derived from Old Welsh is quintessentially Celtic. Dylan appears in the Mabinogi (see page 16).

Sir Walter Scott (from the word *Scotti* given to the invading Irish Celts who settled on the west coast of Scotland) wrote about the conflicts between the old Scottish culture and the English. His most famous story is *Ivanhoe*.

Much more recently Scotland has produced gritty writers, such as Irvine Welsh (meaning 'foreigner' or 'non-Anglo-Saxon'), author of *Trainspotting*, and Jimmy Boyle (descendant of Baoithgheall) the former gangster who developed a passion for writing in prison and produced *A Sense of Freedom*.

Other prominent Celtic surnames in literature include the American essayist Washington Irving (derived from a place in Ayrshire, meaning green river), English thriller writer Frederick Forsyth (meaning mound of fairies, or man of peace or honour), Herman Melville (descendant of Maoilmhichil), author of *Moby Dick*, and F Scott Fitzgerald (an Irish name of Norman origins, meaning son of the spear ruler).

Celtic names in entertainment

Among the list of stars of stage and screen are numerous actors with Celtic names, all touched by the Celtic love of drama. Prominent among them are two James Bonds, Sean Connery (derived from the Irish Conroy, which comes from Cú Raoi, meaning hound of the plain) and the most recent incumbent Daniel Craig (from the Gaelic 'creag', meaning rock). Connery, despite having made his name playing a quintessentially English spy, is a proud Scotsman who is quoted as saying, 'I am not an Englishman, I was never an Englishman, and I don't ever want to be one. I am a Scotsman! I was a Scotsman and I will always be one.'

Among the younger generation of Scottish actors are Ewan McGregor (son of Griogar), who rose to fame in *Trainspotting* and went on to play the young Obi-Wan Kenobi in the prequel trilogy of *Star Wars*, and James McAvoy (a variant of McEvoy, meaning son of *fiodhbhadhach*, the woodman), who starred in *The Last King of Scotland* and *Atonement*.

Celtic names proliferate among Hollywood stars both past and present. Ben Affleck (a place name in Scotland), Matt Damon (from Daman, meaning little stag), Robert Downey Jr (descendant of Dúnadhach, the fortress holder), Keira Knightley (Keira is a variant of Ciara, meaning dark), Colin Firth (from a place in Scotland, or from the Welsh *fridd*, meaning barren), Charlie Sheen (descendant of 'Síodhachán', the peaceful one), Robin Williams (a common Welsh name meaning son of William).

Monroe is a Scottish name of uncertain origin, sometimes used as a first name for boys. But, of course, it was the assumed name of Norma Jean Baker, aka Marilyn Monroe. But there was nothing assumed about the name James Dean (descendant of the deacon), that other immortalized film star of the 1950s.

The name of Errol Flynn (descendant of Flann, the redhead) lives on as one of the biggest stars of the 1930s and 1940s, the swashbuckling hero of films like *Captain Blood* and *The Adventures of Robin Hood*. Fans of the silent movie genre will point to Harold Lloyd (from the Welsh Llwyd, meaning the grey-haired one) as one of the three greats, alongside Charlie Chaplin and Buster Keaton (possibly from a Cornish word for a settlement).

The horror genre would not have been the same without Vincent Price (son of Rhys, the ardent one), whose moustachioed face adorned such films as *The Pit and the Pendulum* and *Theatre of Blood*, and whose sinister voice featured in Michael Jackson's *Thriller*.

I have listed a mere handful here, but the list goes on. Next time you go to the movies, watch the credits closely and see how many Celtic names you can identify.

Celtic names in music

The Celtic spirit and identity has been preserved through song, the folk music of the Celtic regions still enthusiastically maintained today. In addition, the Celtic love of music and lyrical expression is evident in the names responsible for much of the music of the last 50 years, from Johnny Cash (from the Gaelic 'cais', meaning crooked) to Mary Hopkin (son or daughter of Robert; 'Hob' was a nickname for Robert).

Pop stars that have emerged from Ireland include the Nolan Sisters (descendant of Nuallán, the noble one), Sinead O'Connor (descendant of Conchobhar), Shane McGowan (an anglicized form of Mac Gabhann, meaning son of the smith), the lead singer of the Pogues, Van Morrison (a Scottish name meaning son of Morris) and Daniel O'Donnell (descendant of Domhnall, ruler of the world).

From Scotland we've had Annie Lennox (a Scottish place name from the Gaelic Leamhanach, meaning elm field), Bobby Gillespie (an Anglicized form of Mac Gille Easbuig, meaning servant of the bishop) and Edwin Collins (descendant of Coileán, or young dog), Celtic names that stand out amidst a large number of Scottish bands that took pride in their Celtic identity.

The Welsh are particularly renowned for their singing prowess. Tom Jones may not sound like a Celtic name, but Jones was a name assumed by a large number of Welshmen, from the biblical John, and the surname Jones is a clear indication of Welsh descent. Bryn Terfel, the great bass-baritone, has a very Celtic name, Bryn meaning small hill, Terfel meaning 'oak prince' or 'stubborn prince'.

Where the Irish, Welsh and Scots have migrated elsewhere in the world, they have taken their love of music with them. Some of the biggest names in English popular music have signified Celtic origins. Two such names spring immediately to mind: John Lennon (descendant of Lonán, the little blackbird) and Paul McCartney (from the Gaelic Mac Artaine, meaning son of Artan, the little bear). Johnny Rotten, lead singer of the Sex Pistols, later reverted to his real name, John Lydon (an Irish name meaning descendant of Loideán). Morrissey (from the Gaelic Muirgheas, meaning sea action) decided to drop his first name Stephen and make his career under his Celtic surname alone. From the same city as Morrissey, Manchester, came Oasis, fronted by the brothers Noel and Liam Gallagher (descendant of Gallchobhair, the foreign helper).

Whatever your taste in music, there have been Celtic names that stand out in just about every genre. For country fans there's Glen Campbell (from 'cam' and 'beul', meaning crooked mouth); for lovers of 1970s pop there was David Cassidy (descendant of Caiside, the curly haired one); rock and roll had Eddie Cochran (a Scottish place name) and Jerry Lee Lewis (also a Scottish place name, or possibly derived from the Celtic god Lugh).

Celtic pioneers

Just as the Celts broke new ground as they spread across Europe, many of the greatest advances in human endeavour have been associated with Celtic names.

In 1962 America achieved a major breakthrough in the space race when they succeeded in sending a manned spacecraft to orbit the Earth. That man was John Glenn (a Gaelic name meaning from the valley). Seven years later they scored the biggest victory of all over their Soviet adversaries in putting a man on the moon. His name: Neil Armstrong (an Anglicized form of an Irish Gaelic name meaning son of the strong man). The Celts had made it to the moon!

Meanwhile, back down on Earth, a British polar exploration team had been less successful in their bid to be first to reach the South Pole. Nevertheless, their Terra Nova expedition of 1912 became legendary, as did the man who led it, Captain Robert Falcon Scott (from the Irish *Scotti*).

A pioneer of a different kind was the Scotsman John Logie Baird (bard or poet), whom we have to thank for inventing the television. His fellow Scotsman Alexander Graham Bell (a common Scottish surname of various possible origins) is credited with having invented the telephone. Then there was Charles MacIntosh (son of the chief), inventor of the waterproof coat and John Boyd Dunlop (a Highland Scottish place name, possibly meaning muddy fort), who pioneered the development of the pneumatic tyre.

Another inventor of sorts was Robert Baden-Powell (son of Hywel, the eminent one), the inventor of the Boy Scout movement.

Celtic names in power

At time of writing, the British Prime Minister is David Cameron ('hooked nose'). He succeeded Scotsman Gordon Brown (an Anglicized equivalent of the Gaelic 'donn' for someone with brown hair), who had succeeded Tony Blair (from the Scottish Gaelic *blàr*, meaning from the plain).

In the United States, Celtic names have sat in the Oval Office on many occasions: Bill Clinton (from the Anglicized McClinton, meaning son of the servant of Saint Fintán), Ronald Reagan (descendant of Riagán, the furious or impulsive one) and, of course, from the most famous American political dynasty of them all, John F Kennedy (ironically meaning ugly head).

One of America's most celebrated military leaders, the man who commanded US forces in the crucial Pacific theatre during World War II, was Douglas MacArthur (son of Arthur, the bear).

And one of the most powerful men in the world today is the Australian media mogul Rupert Murdoch (from *muireadhach*, meaning mariner).

Celtic names proliferate in all walks of life, as this small handful of examples highlights. When you start looking for them, you come to realize just how influential the Celtic heritage continues to be. A list of the world's leading brands will include McDonald's, Apple Macintosh, JP Morgan, Merrill Lynch, Kellogg's, Avon and Hennessy – all names that are derived from Celtic origins.

That a culture that had its heyday more than two thousand years ago, that suffered repeated periods of oppression, to the point where it was almost entirely wiped out, should continue to be evidenced so strongly in our time is remarkable, and says a lot about the strength of feeling that the Celtic identity engenders. And while I've picked out some of the more obvious examples of Celtic names in modern life, the fact is that there are hundreds of thousands of Celts whose names have been lost to history, and yet Celts they are, and somewhere deep in their hearts, I suspect they know they are.